The Marketing Over Coffee Playbook:

Now With More Wins and Wrecks!

by John J. Wall

Intro: Now with More Confessions, Disclaimers and Platitudes!..10

Chapter 1: Pure Marketing Gold: Now with More Everything! 15

B2B Marketing..17

Technographics is the New Demographics: 17

How to Get FREE Reconnaissance 17

Tech Event: The One Must-Have................................18

B2B Event Marketing..19

Event Exhibitor Survival Lists 19

Put a Wheel on It 21

If It Breathes, It's Qualified......................................21

ABM v. Customer Journey...22

B2B Email Marketing Pitches....................................23

B2B Emails You Should Never, Ever Send 24

The 3-Link B2B Email 24

An Overlooked B2B Marketing Tactic 25

Email Marketing – Now with More Hygiene and Integration! 26

Vendor Flame-Out Must-Dos and File Transferring Hacks 26

Email List Cleaning 26

Cool Email/Store Integration 28

Advertising..28

In Podcasts We Trust..28

Advertising on Pandora 29

Programmatic Bidding for Ad Space: Waterfall v. Header Bidding 29

"WTF is ads.txt?" 31

How to Evaluate Social Media Influencers 32

Micro Influencers: How to Find & Leverage Them Cost-Effectively 32

Website/SEO 35

SEO: It's ALWAYS Back to the Basics.........................35

WordPress PlugIns for Dynamic Content...................36

A Primer on Hero Images 38

Duplicate Content & Libsyn Blogs...............................38

Own Your Web Presence 39

5 Free SEO Chrome Extensions....................................39

Homeless Marketing Topics: Now with More Categorization Failure! 40

Budgeting Fallacy 40

Book Self-Publishing 41

Why Wikipedia is Unhackable 41

So Kid, You Want to Market? 42

Predictive Modeling..43

Source Attribution Trends..43

How to Predict the (Likely) Death of Your New App ..44

Trends in Web Design 45

Chapter 2: Social Media..47

How to Think About Social Media 48

Fan-Based Marketing 48

ROI You Can't Beat: Get on This Train NOW.............49

Recycling Content via Social Media - Does it Work? .49

Facebook 51

Facebook Engagement Stats..51

The Velvet Rope Community: Dark Social 52

Video, Video, Video..53

Facebook Messenger Bots 53
How do you add a bot to Facebook?.....................54
Facebook Live Video 58
Facebook 360 58
Facebook Marketing Hack..59
Twitter 60
Twitter Character Limit..60
Chris's Twitter Insurance Experiment 60
How Does Twitter Beat Facebook?........................61
LinkedIn 62
LinkedIn Hack for Job Hunters 62
Open Candidates Function 63
Use Discretion...63
Videos Rule 64
Pinterest...64
Audience Targeting 64
Snapchat...65
A Business Case for Snapchat?................................65

Chapter 3: How to Use Google Tools 66
Google Analytics 67
User Explorer 67
How to Use GA to Calculate Complex Sale Goal Value . 69
How To Check Every Page For GA & Tag Manager Tags...70
Google Analytics Suite - Google Optimize 70
The Quadrant Review: Web Site Productivity 73
GA Skewing Referral Source 73
Google Tag Manager (GTM) 74

Google Tag Management..74

Google AutoTrack v. Google Tag Manager 75

Google Data Studio 76

Why and How to Build Your Dashboard 76

The Power of Self-Service..77

Google Accelerated Mobile Pages (AMP).................78

Putting Mobile First 78

SEO...79

Prepping for the "New SEO" 79

Chapter 4: Artificial Intelligence & Machine Learning 83

Quick Primer 84

Machine Learning v. Artificial Intelligence (AI)...........84

AI: The Major Players..86

Machine Intelligence Vendor Chart 87

Marketing and AI 88

What Marketers Can Do Now......................................88

Marketing Analytics AI Framework 89

The New SEO is Machine Learning 90

Natural Language Interpretation: The Screenless Revolution...90

What Watson Can Do For Marketers...........................92

Watson Analytics...93

Watson Digital Marketing 93

Watson Analytics for Social Media..............................93

Watson Visual Recognition 93

MoC What-If: Can John Retire? 94

Chris' AI Press Release Experiment 95

Marketers Need Technologists 96

Cool and Practical Stuff AI Can Do Now 97

Google Translate 98

AI Milestone: KITT vs. Terminator...................98

Donut-Free Cops 99

AI: 1, Medical Doctors: 0 99

Site-Based Marketing 99

Baseball 99

Audition 100

Cardiac Monitoring..................................100

AI Is Far From Perfect *101*

AI Is Far From Safe.................................*102*

The Human Cost.....................................*103*

CMOs Are Not Ready 103

AI and Marketing Jobs Long-Term 103

Beyond Marketing: Looking at the Larger Economy 105

AI for President? 106

Chapter 5: Virtual Reality **107**

Getting Started......................................107

Coming Soon to an Arcade Near You 108

VR: Getting Fit and Other Tips 108

Can VR Outperform Bars or Couch Viewing?..........109

Two Fun, Easy VR Experiences 109

Chapter 6: Apps We Like..........................**111**

Business Apps..111

Travel Apps 119

Home & Recreation 122

All-Around Useful....................................128

Chapter 7: Gear We Like aka Nerds R Us **133**

Headphones/Headsets 133

Makes Life Easier 135

Personal & Home Tech 136

Gearhead Picks..141

Chapter 8: Stuff We Like (And We're Not Paid to Promote) **143**

Cool Random Stuff 144

Doing Well By Doing Good 144

Star Trek White Noise Generator....................145

Insider Shopping Tip 145

Little Known Purple One Recordings................145

A Great Amazon Troll.....................................146

Now With More Voting!...................................146

Media and Ads We Like.................................146

Watch-Worthy Ads...146

Not Fake Media 147

Tech 148

How to: Python 148

Plugins We Like...148

Schneier On Security 149

Internet of Things Hacking Attack 149

The Gartner Hype Cycle 150

Amazon Drone Delivery..................................151

Travel Hacks..151

Airline Hacks 151

Where to Stay 151

Where to Meet 151

Books We Like 152

Chapter 9: Now with More Interviews!..................**158**

The Visionaries.......................................*160*

Seth Godin...160

Simon Sinek 170

Christopher S. Penn 175

David Meerman Scott.........................183

Nick Westergaard 185

Marketing Luminaries *189*

Kipp Bodnar, HubSpot........................189

Scott Brinker, ChiefMarTech.com............193

Allison MacLeod, Rapid7 198

Seiya Vogt, Boxed (formerly of Bitly) 212

Justin Mares, FOMO.com, also Kettle & Fire 219

Social Media, PR and Alternative Media Experts *224*

Jeremy Goldman 224

Tim Street 227

Tom Webster 231

Customer Perception Virtuosos *235*

Jay Baer 235

Kate Edwards.....................................243

Daniel Lemin......................................248

Bonus Chapter - AI Goofs **252**

Intro: Now with More Confessions, Disclaimers and Platitudes!

Marketing Over Coffee (www.MarketingOverCoffee.com) has been running as a podcast for 11 years now, delving into all things caught in the intersection of Marketing and Technology. To keep things interesting (to me, anyway), we also foray into the worlds of music, cool electronics, and other geekery.

7 years ago we came up with the idea of putting some of the show content in print. The 2011 Q4 Marketing Over Coffee Quarterly Review actually did well, but the work of putting it together was more than we could handle. How did getting the best content in to print come back to life?

Confession #1: I Was Book-Shamed

Carol Meinhart, my co-author, and I go way back to when we both worked for an events marketing company. If we ever run into each other over drinks, ask me about the events world back in the day.

While one of MoC's first fans, Carol is probably best described as the loyal opposition.

Carol:

"Great stuff. But people listen to MoC at the wheel, or on the treadmill, or holding a leash. How are they going to use this stuff?"

"Could your show notes be any more cryptic?"

"Your newsletter is only slightly better."

And finally

"I'll show you what a book could look like."

And she did.

Confession #2: Heavier on the B2B Side

Well, sure, the B2B world is where Chris and I spend most of our time. But you'll still find stuff that's applicable to B2C. (And the Gear reccos, App list, and Homeless Marketing Topics apply to everyone.)

Confession #3: Shameless Plugs and Affiliate Links Included

I currently work for EventHero (http://www.EventHero.io) and Chris has his own gig at Trust Insights (https://TrustInsights.ai).

But this confession is the only place where we reference our employers gratuitously; we sprinkle useful examples (Tier 3 start-up anyone?) throughout the book.

Affiliate Links to Amazon: Use them. Frequently, please.

It's a Twitter World

We toyed with the idea: "what if we wrote the book as one long Twitter thread?"

But then we probably couldn't charge for it. And my kids still need to go to college.

So we compromised, using as few words, even as few syllables, as possible. Sentence fragments? Yes!

Grammarians and AP Style Fanatics: Fugeddaboutit.

Quotes Are Not Exact

But they're close. We paraphrased to make some things easier to understand.

Take nothing as 100% true, correct or up-to-date (in other words, nothing here is guaranteed to be accurate or advice of any kind, aka call off your attorneys.)

Stuff That Changed a LOT

This book is based loosely on three years worth of podcasts including some 2018 stuff, just to make sure we included our most recent gear and app fetishes.

A LOT of stuff has changed, especially with technology and social media. We updated a lot of info. But we're pretty sure there will be some things out of date. So, remember, search engines and company web sites are still your friends.

And Stuff That Hasn't Changed

You still need to get the basics done. Facebook advertising, Google tools, even basic SEO are still undone by some marketers.

And anything having to do with human nature is eternal, i.e. don't miss our Interviews chapter.

(Sincere) Platitudes

Special thanks to MoC guests for sharing their time, insights and know-how. And special thanks to my co-host Christopher S. Penn, for sharing the MoC marquee, and for his unflagging data-based orientation. (I submit as evidence Chris's "So Kid, You Want to Market?" section in the Marketing chapter.)

And HUGE thanks to the MoC podcast listeners and sponsors. It's an honor and privilege to share our lessons and discussions with you. Thanks for your continued support and indulging our gear fetish - we will keep delivering the shows!

And if you're not listening to the Marketing Over Coffee podcast - welcome! Join us anytime at www.MarketingOverCoffee.com. We've got 11 years of archived podcasts, including our most popular ones. You can also subscribe to us on iTunes.

Disclaimers aka Call Off Your Attorney

We are not lawyers, financial experts or your marketing team; do not rely on any of our advice. We are not liable for anything you fail at or are stupid about. We are going to try and get you to pay us money for stuff. By viewing our website, listening to our podcast or reading our other materials you agree that we can resell your attention and/or contact information. There is no privacy, actual or implied.

Quotes are not exact. We've taken a lot of liberties with exact quotes. No journalists on this team - just marketers!

We have no consistent or known journalistic style. We write it the way you'd want to read it.

Acknowledgements

This book is dedicated to my Dad. He taught me that nothing matters more than persistence. Do your duty, but be sure to make time for music.

Thank you to the lovely Carin. What the heck happened? Since the last book there are now two little people that have taken over our house. Our adventure continues with a tiny version of me that traveled to the future to save me, and a Saturday Night Live cast member.

If not for Christopher Penn, my podcasting would still be just me trying to be Don Imus. Thanks for working with me to carve out our own corner of the Internet, with coffee.

Thank you to Carol Meinhart for diving into a gigantic pile of rubble to find the gold. The only reason you're not on the cover is because you told me not to put you there.

Thanks to Nory Meinhart, the Mistress of Bitly links and app research. Go and take the Gen Z glory that is bequeathed to you in the business world.

Chapter 1: Pure Marketing Gold: Now with More Everything!

B2B Marketing
>   Technographics is the New Demographics: How to Get FREE Reconnaissance
>   Tech Event: The One Must-Have

B2B Event Marketing
>   Event Exhibitor Survival Lists
>   Put a Wheel on It
>   If It Breathes, It's Qualified
>   ABM v. Customer Journey
>   B2B Email Marketing Pitches
>   B2B Emails You Should Never, Ever Send
>   The 3-Link B2B Email
>   An Overlooked B2B Marketing Tactic

Email Marketing – Now with More Hygiene and Integration!
>   Vendor Flame-Out Must-Dos and File Transferring Hacks
>   Email List Cleaning
>   Cool Email/Store Integration

Advertising
>   In Podcasts We Trust
>   Advertising on Pandora
>   Programmatic Bidding for Ad Space: Waterfall v. Header Bidding
>   "WTF is ads.txt?"
>   How to Evaluate Social Media Influencers
>   Micro Influencers: How to Find & Leverage Them Cost-Effectively

Website/SEO
>   SEO: It's ALWAYS Back to the Basics
>   WordPress PlugIns for Dynamic Content

A Primer on Hero Images
>   Duplicate Content & Libsyn Blogs

Own Your Web Presence
5 Free SEO Chrome Extensions
Homeless Marketing Topics: Now with More Categorization Failure!
Budgeting Fallacy
Book Self-Publishing
Why Wikipedia is Unhackable
So Kid, You Want to Market?
Predictive Modeling
Source Attribution Trends
How to Predict the (Likely) Death of Your New App
Trends in Web Design

You're probably just like us: simultaneously thrilled and horrified that almost every part of marketing gets completely destroyed and rebuilt about every 10 years.

This motley collection of advice, tips and resources can help you navigate the post-apocalyptic marketing landscape, so you can spend more time wearing one shoulder pad and hanging out with Tina Turner (those of you too young to get the reference, see "Mad Max: Beyond Thunderdome") https://www.imdb.com/title/tt0089530/

If you're still confused about what this book is about, it means you didn't read the intro. Get on that before going ahead.

B2B Marketing

Technographics is the New Demographics:

How to Get FREE Reconnaissance

Technography sounds complicated, but it's not. It's the measure of a company's number and type of tech solutions (i.e. a quick, useful handle on a prospect's or customer's technology landscape.)

FREE: To get intelligence on a prospect's or customer's stack, install the Ghostery and BuiltWith plugins on your browser (they're both free). Ghostery reveals the ad tracking systems used by a site, for example publishers commonly use DoubleClick. BuiltWith shows the solutions the site is running.

If you see solutions that require a large investment, like Salesforce, you can deduce that the company has the resources to pony up the funds to invest in your solution. If you're selling a large enterprise solution, and a company can't afford $300 a seat for Salesforce, there's no way they're going to drop $500k on your solution.

Here's a summary of ways to use technography to get market intelligence, and to sell solutions more effectively:

- Mention relevant integrations in any upcoming pitches (for example: your solution integrates with Salesforce and other popular enterprise solutions)

17

- Determine if a company has made investment in high-priced, enterprise solutions

- Jump in if you see that a customer is testing competitive software. This sleuthing technique works only with SaaS software. You can see when new code has been added to your customer's website that feeds a SaaS application. For example, you could look at the code behind signup forms to identify which solutions are getting the data.

Good article on how to use refined technography info to sell solutions based on a prospect's stack: http://bit.ly/2nAc90H

Tech Event: The One Must-Have

Chris and John have strong opinions on the staff you need to bring if you're exhibiting at a tech event. Feel free to show this part of the book to any exec who's concerned about the investment in sending a non-marketing staffer to tech events.

Chris: "At most marketing shows, I can forgive a marketing vendor who brings the average salesperson. We need business users learning about marketing technology for the space to survive and thrive. But if you're exhibiting at a marketing technology show and you fail to bring a technology person to work at your booth, you have failed. And you've reduced your credibility to exactly zero.

"I had a conversation with a vendor at a booth recently, and I could tell he was reciting from the script in his head: 'We employ the latest artificial intelligence tools to make your content marketing resonate emotionally with your audience.'

To be fair to the sales rep, his company threw them to the wolves. It's not the sales rep's job to know the technology."

John: "Make sure there's at least one product manager at the show. There's a ton of people on the show floor that don't know exactly what they're looking for and they could use the remedial education. But more importantly, you need to have at least a product manager for anyone who wants to ask hardcore, technical questions.

"To help justify the expense, the product manager can also be working on BusDev partnerships. If a $1M+ prospect at the show wants some real details, you'll have got the right person on-hand to answer the question and develop the relationship."

B2B Event Marketing

Event Exhibitor Survival Lists

John and Sean Zinsmeister of ThoughtSpot shared some of their tried-and-true exhibitor and event-going hacks during a recent Dreamforce event.

Sean: "Smaller 'side-on' events, usually sponsored by vendors, tend to have the best content, the best food, and the most engaged audiences. Hunt for them on the conference program. Also, try to get on the vendor's list of presenters, so you can network more effectively with the attendees."

John: "Don't automatically invest in a full conference badge. You can put together meetings and schedule meals with tons of people in your network, both pre-show and during the show."

Don't leave home without these show must-haves:

- Comfortable Shoes

- Charger(s)

- Mints (when in doubt, share)

- American Express Platinum Card (pricey, but gets you into the flight clubs)

- Laptop (the lightest one you can afford)

- 10-12 hours of books, movies or TV on your iPad or laptop

- Small flashlight

- Black Sharpie

- Business cards

- A $50 bill (hidden outside your wallet - in case you lose your wallet)

- 2-ft headphone cord

John's classic book, "B2B Marketing Confessions" has a full list of supplies to pack into the show-going crate and other unusual trade show advice, along with other can't miss B2B marketing info. If you're a B2B marketer, drop $10 on the Kindle edition: https://amzn.to/2pRwtvV

Put a Wheel on It

At a recent Dreamforce (Salesforce's annual mega-event), Sean Zinsmeister noted that drones are a big giveaway item. Vendors have also stepped up their on-site marketing by offering one-shot experiences, like a ride in a Formula One race car.

But the one thing that keeps bringing the booth traffic? Wheels. It's amazing how many people will line up at a booth to spin a wheel. Most of the time the prize for a spin is a small gift card, but attendees love to walk away with something, no matter what the vendor is pitching at the show.

If It Breathes, It's Qualified

John: "At Dreamforce, pretty much everyone is qualified. Keep in mind that even if you're an exhibitor, the show producer isn't necessarily going to give or sell you a list of attendees that you can bombard afterward. It's a worthy goal to get as many badge scans as possible.

"When I've analyzed data from past events, I found that everyone attending was qualified. We found that we'd get more than 50% of our deals from generic badge scans done while walking the floor; not everyone makes it over to the booth. (And of course, I'd be remiss if I didn't plug EventHero as the best lead retrieval system going!)

"I knew a company that scammed badge scans by standing at the front of the lunch line, claiming that people had to have their badges scanned to get fed."

Sean (while working at Infer): "We equipped our sales reps with a mobile app called Dreamforce Hunger Games. The apps are plugged into the Infer API, and there's a spiff that we develop for every show, but the SDRs walk the show floor, enter an attendee's email address into the mobile and then the app walks you through the simulation. It's an easy conversation starter.

"People forget that exhibitors are often prospects. Your reps can walk booth-to-booth, and exchange pitch-for-pitch, to grab prospects. (If you integrate this activity into InsightSquared, there's a live dashboard that will show you where all the A leads on the floor are coming from.)"

John: "There's rarely a decision maker at the booth, but you can definitely come up with a list of companies. Also, at Dreamforce, a vendor that's able to afford a 10x10 booth is a proxy for having budget for marketing and software."

ABM v. Customer Journey

Because both terms are hot, some vendors have taken some creative license when updating their marketing message and collateral. (Instead of Customer Journey, some companies also use the term Customer Experience, or the acronym CX.)

Chris: "Customer Journey is usually an inconvenient construct for the marketer because there aren't clear answers, role divisions, and the metrics are muddy until you see the macro picture.

Marketing funnels are for marketers, journeys are for customers, and maybe there will be a happy medium somewhere. But if you are truly dedicated to the customer journey and the customer experience, your life as a marketer will be miserable."

Customer Journey is NOT the marketing funnel. Customer Journey is a data-driven phenomenon, which requires the right analytics tools and methodology. Note: if analytics are not your organization's strong suit, or you're short on time, talk to Chris about Trust Insights. They not only map the customer path, but also forecast when customers will come down the path: http://bit.ly/2OzSqdg

The biggest differentiator between the two:

Marketing Funnel - is built for the convenience of the marketer

Customer Journey - is built for the convenience of the customer (when built correctly)

B2B Email Marketing Pitches

John on B2B email: "There seems to be the 'flavor of the month' approach to B2B email. The messaging can vary from 'person pitch' ('Who is the right person at your company to contact?') to the 'minutes' pitch ('I know you're busy, but if you only have 15 minutes, let's talk'). John says that if you come up with something new and novel, you may do well for the first 3 days of using that pitch. Afterward, everyone will start to copy you, and your clever approach will die a quick death, both for you and your imitators."

John is astonished that B2B marketers still send mass email blasts. He says: "The way to do it in B2B is to create a standard email body, but always open up with customized content that shows some knowledge of the potential customer. Ideally, you want to include a link to relevant information that ties very tightly to the customer. Above all, you need an individual hook for each email. If you don't do that, and continue to send mass emails, you run the risk of getting blocked from the recipient's in-box."

B2B Emails You Should Never, Ever Send

John: "This email kills me the most: 'I was just wondering if you had a chance to follow up on my previous emails.'"

Chris files an email with this subject line in the trash bin:

"Re: Re: Re: our software discussion"

(i.e. A subject line with multiple Re:'s: when there's been no prior email discussion)

Note: Gmail doesn't append a "re:" to a reply anymore, so if you were toying with this idea, DON'T DO IT.

The 3-Link B2B Email

John: "One thing I've seen that has worked somewhat well is sending an email with 'decision' links in it. The body copy reads something like this: 'Look, I've sent you two or three emails. I don't want to bother you. Please just click on one of these links.'

Link 1: Click here if you'd never buy this

Link 2: Click here if you're interested; contact me

Link 3: Click here if it isn't the right time, but you want to keep getting occasional emails"

The upside of this copy is that it's "one and done." You're not asking the recipient to go through the heavy lifting of composing a reply. Instead of getting ignored, you're more likely to get a useful response (especially if one of the links is 'never bother me again' - not chasing after the deadwood is a win-win for everyone.)

Chris put this email format through his marketing automation system, setting up 3 different landing pages (yes, no and maybe), so he can track the clicks to each landing page by URL. He then uses the response to adjust the recipient's lead score up or down.

An Overlooked B2B Marketing Tactic

Chris: "One of the marketing tactics that's worked very well is sending a physical package by express mail to senior management. We've found that most administrative assistants won't open a package addressed directly to the exec. We're going to try an even more upscale version of the same approach."

John agrees: "Sending physical pieces in overnight mail boxes is expensive, so it can be a hard sell to senior management, who are spoiled by the cost of ultra cheap email. But because receiving physical packages in an office is so rare, your package may become a water-cooler event, especially if you dress up the box. Don't be afraid to put things like your logo, creative copy, and novel stuff on the box. The big question here: Are you going to 'spray and pray' (email), or identify your top 10 prospects and market to them uniquely?"

Email Marketing – Now with More Hygiene and Integration!

Vendor Flame-Out Must-Dos and File Transferring Hacks

You probably have a plan for updating and cleaning your email list, but what about making sure your list is safe in case of an email marketing vendor shut down or buy out? If and when you change email marketing vendors (because you'll switch vendors at least once in your career), you need to take these preventative steps:

Chris: "Once per quarter, export your past creative and lists into backup media. Cloud storage is fine. You never want your email lists to be at the mercy of a vendor; they can be sold, shut down or quit operations for any reason."

John: "Once a year, do a full restore of any email lists and creative that you've backed up. You should actually grab the backed up data and load it into some marketing email software, and make sure that everything will restore. That's the best way to make sure your email marketing assets haven't been destroyed or are inaccessible for any reason."

Email List Cleaning

John has been has been impressed by Bounceless.io for list cleaning. Chris used Amazon Simple Email Service (Amazon SES) as a back-up server when switching email platforms. Side benefit: it appears that Amazon may be better at identifying bad addresses and list cleaning than some commercial solutions. Chris found that that he got a surprisingly high volume of email bounces after his Amazon back-up and first email send.

Amazon provides a ton of email stats:

- Status Messages

- Bounce Rate Notification

- Complaint Rate Notification

- Anti-Spam Organization Notification

- Direct Feedback Notification

- Domain Blocklist Notification

- Internal Review Notification

- Mailbox Provider Notification

- Recipient Feedback Notification

- Related Account Notification

- Spamtrap Notification

- Vulnerable Site Notification

- Other Notification

For more information on Amazon's smorgasbord of stats:

https://amzn.to/2Mqlfv2

A few cautions: Some email service providers, after 3 - 4 bounces, will mark an email address as inactive. Also, your email provider's servers may blacklist addresses, whether merited or not.

Depending on how big the undeliverables file is, it may be worthwhile to run it through another email service (a disposable account because odds are you're going to have a terrible delivery rate and you don't want to hurt your sender reputation on your primary account). You would want to test them in small batches to see if it's worth the effort or not. If the original email service provider has done their hygiene right it's probably not worth doing. Conversely, when you change email marketing providers/servers, you might find that emails that your system judged to be undeliverable may go through and get delivered with your new system.

Cool Email/Store Integration

MailChimp can easily connect your store to MailChimp's email to make product recommendations. You just connect your store to MailChimp, and it will go through your sales data. You'll get a line of code to put in your email template, and they'll insert a recommended product box. That's real marketing automation, taking away the work involved in recommendations via email. https://blog.mailchimp.com/introducing-product-recommendations/

Advertising

In Podcasts We Trust

After 12+ years in podcasting, with 2 podcasts going out every week (www.MarketingOverCoffee.com and www.StackandFlow.com), John is definitely biased toward podcasting.

But, as it turns out, with good reason: This article from Adweek http://bit.ly/2OBKrMN is a short look at why podcasts are the preferred medium for advertising. You've got to love podcasts because ads are routinely skipped only 25% of the time. So give advertising in podcasts a shot -John knows a couple of great marketing-related ones ;-)

Advertising on Pandora

Some music genres survive long past their pop culture shelf life; artists and bands that were popular decades ago still have tremendous pull. Test advertising on Pandora if you want to generate traffic from certain profiles that match with the demographics of the music listeners.

Great article from Adweek: http://bit.ly/2Bb5dks

Programmatic Bidding for Ad Space: Waterfall v. Header Bidding

If a ton of your ad budget is spent on online advertising, or if you're a publisher seeking to maximize revenues from online ads, it behooves you to understand the difference between Header Bidding v. Waterfall bidding.

Here's our take on how programmatic bidding for ad space works, and how header bidding looks to be more advantageous than waterfall bidding.

Programmatic bidding is all about how ad servers choose what ads to show. There are two basic models: Waterfall and Header Bidding.

Waterfall model: Waterfall bidding is been the traditional, fallback model of bidding for ad space. A publisher's "must run" house ads get first priority. Then ad servers kick in: the subsequent slots come up for bid in order: 2nd slot, 3rd slot, and onward. The ads are served as the web page loads, hence, the term waterfall.

Header bidding: In a model called The Open Air Auction, the house ad is still served first. But then the remaining slots are put up for bid, simultaneously and automatically. Let's say there are 5 positions on an ad page, and there's one house ad. The house ad gets the top slot. Then, 4 ad servers are taking bids for each slot simultaneously. The highest bidder gets slot number 2, the next highest bidder gets slot number 3, and the lowest bidder gets slot number 4. And all this bidding happens within 200 +/- milliseconds, so it's undetectable to the viewer.

Publishers benefit from header bidding because it opens up the opportunity for greater profitability, because there's simultaneous bidding for open inventory at the same exact time.

Marketers get a better shot at ad inventory because they can run bids for all available slots. If bidding via a network, a marketer gets only one of the slots, because waterfall bidding is sequential rather than the simultaneous bidding for ad slots in header bidding. For example, a marketer bidding via a network could be the unlucky soul who gets the 150 x 50 or tiny banner at the bottom page - paying for views, but not necessarily anything else."

Does Waterfall bidding have any advantages? Pages with Waterfall bidding may allow a page to serve faster (due to the lack of auction movement behind the scenes).

For more detail on Waterfall v. Header Bidding, check out these Digiday articles provided to us at the recommendation of Marc Goldberg, CEO of Trust Metrics (www.TrustMetrics.com):

"Amazon Pitches Publishers a New Header Bidding Wrapper"

http://bit.ly/2MpFAAS

This article from MarketingLand provides more info and useful illustrations:

https://mklnd.com/2KSpbA1

"WTF is ads.txt?"

https://digiday.com/marketing/wtf-ads-txt/

Caveat: When budgeting for advertising on networks of any kind, remember that ad fraud, mostly due to bots, is real. The Association of National Advertising (ANA) reports that 9% of desktop display and 22% of video spending was fraudulent.

The good news? "Fraud in programmatic media buys is no longer riskier than general market buys as media agencies have improved filtration processes and controls."

Read the rest of the report (it's short and useful): "The Bot Baseline: Fraud in Digital Advertising 2017 Report http://www.ana.net/content/show/id/botfraud-2017

How to Evaluate Social Media Influencers

Chris: "There's a certain mystique to the value of influencers in the marketing mix. While it may seem that they add a degree of glamour to your PR and marketing, what's the right price to pay for celebrity?

"Shift Communications studied the 365-day profiles of 16,000 known influencers. Influencers can generate results, but it boils down to the ROI of shares or clicks. Influencers are an advertising channel, and should be compared to PPC advertising. If you're marketing via influencers, be sure to look at your influencer contracts, especially those based on tiers of service. Look for performance-based marketing; those influencers who aren't confident in their ability to perform will balk at anything other than flat fees, while those influencers who can deliver the goods will be eager to look at bonuses and other performance-based arrangements. Generally, an influencer's performance will be based on a great match between the influencer, the content, and real customers."

For more info: Are Influencers Overpaid? http://bit.ly/2w6qxBV

Micro Influencers: How to Find & Leverage Them Cost-Effectively

A micro-influencer marketing program is an underutilized marketing tactic. If you do a good job selecting of influencers, and you offer a quality produce and/or service, then influencer marketing can transfer loyalty from the influencer to your brand (although you always need to see quantifiable proof - see section "How to Evaluate Social Media Influencers" above.)

An effective influencer marketing program is also a good insurance policy against changes to Google's, Facebook's, and Twitter's algorithms. Instead of subjecting your marketing results to the whims of the search and social media algorithms, influencer marketing (if done right) allows you to gain consistent and reliable audience access.

The challenge is to target a list of influencers based on a mixture of engagement, reach and affordability. Don't just throw darts at a dartboard, chasing after the five celebrities who everybody's trying to pitch. With some analysis, you can identify more targeted, better value B or C list influencers (micro influencers). There are people with 10,000 followers that can provide your brand with more relevant engagement than social media personalities followed by millions.

When deciding between B-list and C-listers, you also need to do the math. Compare 10 C-list influencers who have 10,000 followers against a B-list of influencers at 10 times the price point with 20,000 followers. You're better off scooping up those C influencers.

Also keep in mind that while the A-listers have the industry clout, a lot of B-listers and C-listers are the primary source of content; they "feed" the A-listers. That's another way of getting A-list bang for your B-list or C-list buck.

If you want the best and most recent data on ranking people's influence, you need to do the raw data mining yourself, or find a company like Trust Insights https://TrustInsights.ai (Chris' firm) to do the mining (and possibly add data from public sources) for you.

You'll want to scrape this data:

1. Topical alignment - put together a "Who's Who" list of social media target. Hint: Save yourself some work by using industry-published lists of "Top 10" people to follow on Twitter, etc.

2. Who's got the biggest mouth, i.e. highest number of followers

3. Who has the highest engagement numbers? Click-throughs, retweets, shares, etc. Some people have enormous reach but little engagement.

4. What are the influencers are sharing? To get this info, you'll need pull social media data (e.g. tweets from Twitter) and load it into a machine-learning tool. The data pull will give you an idea of what the influencers are talking about, so you can put together an attractive outreach program.

Chris recommends the machine learning solutions below. Also, the data processing is downright cheap; Chris did a multi-gigabyte data download into BigQuery and got a bill for 24 cents!

Watson Analytics
https://www.ibm.com/watson-analytics

R-Studio
https://www.rstudio.com/

Also, if you have staff who know their way around a data warehouse:

BigQuery
https://cloud.google.com/bigquery/

NoSQL Database
Offered by a number of vendors, including Amazon Web Services
https://aws.amazon.com/nosql/

Website/SEO

SEO: It's ALWAYS Back to the Basics

This SearchEngineWatch article lists the 14 most important SEO tasks, in order of priority http://bit.ly/2vGChLN

It's a terrific Basic SEO checklist if you're working on a new website or refreshing an existing website.

It's not a glamorous list:

1. Identify & remove duplicate content

2. Check if your navigation still works

3. Make sure you have responsive design

4. Set-up Google Analytics and Search Console (formerly known as Webmaster Tools)

5. Create local search accounts in your Maps account

6. Offer only quality content: relevant, timely, fresh and valuable (see note)

7. Make sure you're showing up in Google

But because these tasks are fundamental to successful SEO, and because Google has stamped out all the "tricks," everything else can wait until you get these tasks done.

Note: Item #6 became an additional "must-do" once Google incorporated Panda (its algorithm filtering out poor quality content) into its core algorithm. You should review and remove your worst performing content at least annually. (Worst performing = content with the least views. If views = zero, rewrite or delete the page.) Don't forget to review content like YouTube videos, local map content, etc. Getting rid of the stale, less-than-great stuff will cause your current content to perform better.

Advanced SEO Tip: Anytime you see a downward shift in your SEO results, or Google announces a new update, do a content review-and-purge of your worst performing content.

WordPress PlugIns for Dynamic Content

Chris: "There are WordPress plugins like Insert PHP (https://wordpress.org/plugins/insert-php/) that enable you to natively execute code before publishing a WordPress post. By using these plugins, you can have dynamic content in your posts, but when the content goes to all the downstream sites, it's static code, so your content won't get scraped out or hijacked."

As an example, look at the screenshot (below) of Chris' blog (see it online: http://bit.ly/2MM1CdN)

If you use a code execution plugin, you can use shortcodes to generate dynamic content within your post, such as calls to action or newsletter signup forms. That's the best of both worlds: because the post is calling a shortcode you can make global changes to your calls to action, but also because the execution of the code happens before the post is sent to the browser.

When you turn on AMP or Facebook Instant Articles, if you're using shortcodes to embed your ads in your post, then all your ads go with your post to Facebook Instant Articles. You save your advertising, because none of the site navigation goes with it, only the post content. By using this type of execution plug-in to serve up your ads, you preserve your ad impressions. You might even get the benefit of boosting those particular ads.

If a spammer scraped Chris's post (referring to the screenshot below), without the plugin, they'd get the "Want to read more?" form and the ads for the Blue Belt book and Planning Framework tool. With the plugin, if this content were shared or scraped, his call to actions go along for the ride - Chris is making the spammers do some promotion for him!

A Primer on Hero Images

John is still a fan of old school print principles. If you're into layout and design, you know how important it is to have a great hero image. (A hero image is the largest and most prominent image on a page. The term can apply to either the printed page, or a web page.)

WordStream Blog: http://www.wordstream.com/blog/ws/2016/06/07/hero-images-guide

Duplicate Content & Libsyn Blogs

Libsyn (www.Libsyn.com), a podcasting host, can generate a blog from your content. But to avoid duplicate content - and Google's corresponding punishment - just go into the Libsyn template, and add a "No Follow" meta tag. Google won't follow the Libsyn blog, and you'll still get all the Google juice from your web page/blog. Also, be sure to use the Yoast SEO (www.Yoast.com) plug-in on your main blog and make sure the rel=canonical tag is set ON. The tag will indicate to Google that yours is the canonical, authoritative source for your content - if someone else is scraping your content, Google will reward you in the search rankings, not the scraper.

Own Your Web Presence

Chris: "We're in 'peak social' mode: people have maxed out on spending time on social media. While Facebook is a good way to publish your content, you can't completely rely on Facebook to house and offer your content. Also, Facebook commands a premium in the social media marketplace, so if they decide to charge for any portion of their services, relying on them exposes you to those likely premium-level charges.

"So do not let your media properties go dormant by publishing only on Facebook. You still need your own blog or website, your own newsletter, and your own content. You're always in a much better position if you're an influencer, and you're curating your own audience."

5 Free SEO Chrome Extensions

Searchland found a good set of tools that enable tasks like link-checking, word count, etc:

1. Nimbus Screenshot (Very hot, 1M+ users)

2. Check My Links

3. WordCount

4. Open Multiple URLs - Good

5. NOTE: User Agent Switcher -- Sadly, we believe this may be spyware. We suggest you use the Google version instead: http://bit.ly/2w6xYJr

John checked to make sure they all work. https://selnd.com/2KP6QE7

Homeless Marketing Topics: Now with More Categorization Failure!

Here's a bunch of useful marketing stuff that we could not figure out how to categorize.

Budgeting Fallacy

Chris: "I saw an article and infographic saying the top companies all spend X% of their revenue on marketing. Using an arbitrary "industry" percentage guideline isn't the best way to judge or manage your marketing spend for a few reasons:

"If revenue is weak, and you shrink your marketing spend down to an arbitrary % of revenue, your risk more harm to your top line. Marketing is what drives revenue in the first place."

Chris likes the tool offered by Google to calculate optional AdWords spend; his blog post is worth a read if you use paid search: http://bit.ly/2P4awoF

John advises: "If you have sufficient revenue, you want to take a 'ground-up' approach to your marketing spend by managing to your marketing channels' inflection points (i.e. an additional dollar spent in any given channel has zero-to-little ROI). If you have no historical revenue, or you don't have sufficient revenue, you can try to apply an arbitrary marketing/revenue relationship - but be prepared to break out the Tums."

Book Self-Publishing

You can still publish and promote your book without a big name author. Gumroad is a great site for publishers who price their work below $9.99.

Why the magical price of $9.99? Once the book price exceeds $9.99 on Amazon, the publisher's royalty drops from 70% to 35%. To get the same revenue on Amazon that you'd get from Gumroad, you'd need to increase the cost of the book commensurately (and watch your sales plummet).

Gumroad will provide you with customer transaction detail, including the emails of the book buyers for follow-up or future marketing. (While we love Amazon, it doesn't give the publisher customer data.)

John and Chris are also huge fans of Jay Baer's approach to book marketing. Here's the web site if you want some inspiration for your own publications. http:// www.jaybaer.com/hug-your-haters/

We hope we did Jay proud with our book marketing. See our chapter on Jay's interview and Hug Your Haters in this book.

Why Wikipedia is Unhackable

While working at Shift Communications (a PR firm), Chris discovered that Wikipedia was disallowing changes from Shift. From a technical standpoint, that means that Wikipedia figured out which IP addresses correspond to PR firms, or decided to blacklist certain PR firms from making changes. John has also found that changes submitted to Wikipedia by a company usually get deleted also.

And don't count on making changes through non-company IPs to work either. Changes are monitored by a team of Wikipedia editors; if an editor is vigilant, they'll look up who made the change. If the person that made the change has a history of doing a lot of good Wikipedia work across an array of topics, Wikipedia will most likely accept the change. If the change comes from a single generic account that's only fighting for edits on one company page, that will get smacked down most of the time. You can increase your odds of getting a change through if the account is not generic. But if the editor finds out that the changes come from someone who works at the company via Google/Facebook/LinkedIn, Wikipedia will slap that account down by deleting any edits and even locking a company page to pre-approved editors).

If your C-suite requires specific language on the Wikipedia site, or if your analytics show that Wikipedia is a good source of inbound traffic, you'll have to find a champion of your company who knows Wikipedia (not internal staff or PR firm) to make edits on your behalf.

So Kid, You Want to Market?

Chris: "My wife and daughter wanted to set up an Etsy business, and they asked me: 'How does it work?' They were going to just throw up something on an Etsy page. I told them: 'You've got to market your shop, because the idea of 'build it and they will buy' hasn't worked on the Internet for about 15 years. I started to write notes with marketing pointers and decided to turn it into a blog series."

Editor's note: Chris is being overly modest. His series gives anyone, not just kids, a good primer to starting and running a small online business. Chapters in the series: Intro, Finding a Unique Product, Handling the Money, Marketing Strategy & Tactics, Website Basics, Social Media, Email Marketing, Conclusion

The 8-part series on Chris's blog starts here: http://bit.ly/2MJSKFy

Predictive Modeling

When it comes to predictive analytics, you can't just flip the switch on and expect it to work. You need to keep going back, and turning the knobs and dials to get the model's output to match reality. Until you get the model tuned up, you can't depend on results. It's a constantly iterative process.

When it comes to one-time events, like a product launch, you can't model it. Or as Chris says: "I don't think it's possible to model a Black Swan."

Source Attribution Trends

After attending a CMO Summit, Chris observed that there's a "pendulum effect" when it comes to source attribution. The pendulum swings between the one extreme of demanding very precise, source-related attribution, and the other extreme of focusing on intangibles, like building brand, reputation and trust. When the pendulum swings to the intangibles end, that's the time organizations are willing to invest in activities like advertising, media buys and public relations, because those are the tools that move the pendulum toward intangibles.

Adrian Chang, formerly of Oracle, now at Informatica, was a guest on John's other podcast, Stack and Flow: http://bit.ly/2Mm6hq2

Adrian had an important observation about attribution. He advises to not lose sleep over first or last touch, because it's system driven. He also suggests keeping your models flexible, and even use multiple models, because the key to results isn't measuring finite promotions (trying to line up exactly where every action comes from). It's more important to identify the 2 - 3 things that signify that the prospect is going to buy.

How to Predict the (Likely) Death of Your New App

Unless your app is closely connected to your brand, like the MoC app (a screaming bargain at only $1.99 that provides access all episodes https://apple.co/2BjLWNZ) you're at the mercy of the app marketplace.

According to Chris, if you crack the list of top apps, and then fall out of that list within a week, your odds of re-entry are almost zero. Once you get enough exposure to crack the top 50-100, your user experience has to be so good that people immediately start recommending your app to colleagues and friends.

Here's a link to "App Annie," which shows the top 50 free, paid, and revenue grossing iOS apps https://www.appannie.com/en/apps/ios/top/

An app may have a few cool features and gain some traction. Or an app can be the entry point to a significant business such as Tinder and Snapchat.

If your app is good enough, Facebook may attempt one of two tactics: 1. Attempt to buy your app/business and/or 2. Seek to emulate your app's core capabilities. An example would be Facebook's intent to pursue an app-based dating venture (announced in mid-2018).

Keep in mind that a new app has to have a significant aspect or capability that cannot be copied easily. Google put all its financial and marketing might against Facebook with Google+, and Google+ never got the traction it needed. If Google can't win against Facebook, who can?

Another piece of app development advice: "Be wary of building apps in China or with sources where there may be questionable coding practices. It's too easy to sneak in hostile code."

Trends in Web Design

Web design is just becoming more complicated and difficult. Mobile has wiped out everything. You have to deal with all kinds of platforms, different use cases, and geography issues. The number of platforms has exploded: web, desktop, mobile, tablet, smartphone, in-app, Google AMP, and Facebook Instant articles.

Soon, we'll add virtual reality, augmented reality and microscreens (tiny screens like the Apple Watch) to the design mix. It's not surprising that confusing technologies, the number of vendors, and the potential for things to go wrong design-wise increases each time you add a new piece of technology to the stack.

There's also a move to better quality photos (good-bye to stock photos), and progressive apps are important, as people want to get around the Apple Store. John recommends these Noupe.com articles:

http://bit.ly/2B5Uvvm

http://bit.ly/2B5WLDa

http://bit.ly/2nBI2pZ

Chapter 2: Social Media

How to Think About Social Media
    Fan-Based Marketing
    ROI You Can't Beat: Get on This Train NOW
    Recycling Content via Social Media - Does it Work?
Facebook
    Facebook Engagement Stats
    The Velvet Rope Community: Dark Social
    Video, Video, Video
    Facebook Messenger Bots
    How do you add a bot to Facebook?
    Facebook Live Video
    Facebook 360
    Facebook Marketing Hack
Twitter
    Twitter Character Limit
    Chris's Twitter Insurance Experiment
    How Does Twitter Beat Facebook?
LinkedIn
    LinkedIn Hack for Job Hunters
Open Candidates Function
    Use Discretion
    Videos Rule
Pinterest
    Audience Targeting
Snapchat
    A Business Case for Snapchat?

The Social Media landscape changes so fast that our friend, Jason Keath, has been able to do a full-on event about it every year. Whether you're a small business trying to marshal some organic reach, or you're spending $50k/ month to bring in guaranteed leads, here's an overview of what you can do to make your social media more effective.

How to Think About Social Media

Fan-Based Marketing

John hosted Darshan Kaler, CEO & Co-Founder of Tradeable Bits, a fan-based platform for music and sports brands. We like Darshan's take on the true definition and value of social media: "Social media is people using technology to come together on a particular site to propagate their interests. The value is not the content or the activity that occurs. The value is the individual person, recognizing that each person has a different personality on Facebook, Twitter or Instagram.

"To understand advertising on social media, we need to make the distinction between search engine advertising and social media advertising. The basis of advertising is relevancy and recency. For example, when someone searches on Google for info on travel to Hawaii, Google provides real-time information on travel options. It's a very effective advertising model because, by definition, the searcher's interest is 100% recent and relevant. Social media advertising is more of a targeting strategy, with the goal of serving your ad to a social media user whose profile and actions matches your typical customers profile.

"People that buy your product are your fans, and they're talking about your product online, and the size of your company doesn't matter. Companies need to understand: you're no longer simply comparing a customer who spent $500 v. one who spent $30. If someone is an influencer within an online community, regardless of what's spent by the influencer, their positive or negative experience can affect the bottom line. It's not about just the dollars that are being spent, it's also how influential these potential customers are."

ROI You Can't Beat: Get on This Train NOW

Chris wants to remind everyone that if you're not doing Lookalike advertising on social media platforms, YOU ARE MISSING OUT on **online campaign clickthrough rates as high as 30-35%.**

To implement Lookalike advertising you need:

1. A customer list to upload to social media platforms

2. A list of at least 100 people

When you get in front of the right people with the right messages on social media, the results are unbelievable. Chris has seen companies achieve a lookalike campaign clickthrough rate (CTR) as high 35%, while the rest of the company's marketing CTR averages about 1%.

Recycling Content via Social Media - Does it Work?

Chris killed two birds with one stone - he went on vacation AND he recycled content from his blog to share while on break. Luckily for MoC, Chris also used his downtime to perform an interesting social media experiment. Chris recounts:

"I wanted to do a test. In the past, I've identified the top viewed pages on the blog. During my vacation, I wanted to recycle stuff that was sharable, so I ran my blog through a share analysis tool to find the Top 25 most shared blog posts of the current year. Then I syndicated the posts by stuffing them back into Buffer (scheduling tool) and shared them again."

Results:

1. Chris got about a +15% increase in new shares on content that people have already seen and already shared.

2. A surprise: The most popular content shared the first time published was not the most shared content the second time around.

3. Content recycling did produce a 62% increase in traffic from social, but only a .8% increase in overall traffic. That means that a lot of people did mindless sharing without clicking through to read.

The Moral of the story? Yes, you can recycle content to stir up social media activity, but don't count on it to produce actual clicks to your website.

Facebook

Facebook Engagement Stats

If you or your management is counting on organic engagement with Facebook for results, it's a low, low probability game.

How low?

Shift Communications (Chris's former employer) pulled FB engagement rate stats for 57 major B2B and B2C brands for a 12-week period in the summer of 2016 (yes, the data is a little old, but it's still instructive.) Engagement on FB consists of likes, comments and shares.

FB Engagement rate (likes, comments and shares): **.12 - .31%**

(i.e. between 12 - 31 out of every 10,000 people engage with organic Facebook content)

According to Chris: "The data is pretty clear: you'd be better off standing in Times Square yelling at people than using organic, unpaid social on Facebook."

Also, in order to avoid exposing its audience to what may be perceived as potentially biased news reports, even from generally accepted publishers of news, FB has decreased publishers' exposures in timelines, and is increasing exposure to the news of family and friends. If you want to guarantee exposure in Facebook, get out your credit card.

Paper from Shift Communications: http://www.shiftcomm.com/blog/sorry-state-social-media-engagement/

The Velvet Rope Community: Dark Social

A lot of great discussions have moved to "Dark Social": private groups on Facebook, WeChat, SnapChat, and other P-to-P messaging apps. These member-only groups now dominate social media; people tend to spend most of their Facebook time in groups. The "Dark" in Dark Social refers to groups that are not searchable on Google or Facebook.

Outsiders can't access the group's discussion, and you can't even figure out if someone belongs to a private group, because private groups do not show up on Facebook's Groups section.

Some group membership is by invite-only, and you can't buy access to the group. John belongs to a private Facebook group that shares advertising critiques. The group is member-by-invite only, because a lot of it is NSFW (Not Safe For Work, i.e. occasionally foul mouthed).

You'll need to do some work to find the influencers who belong to these private groups. If you're able to identify private groups, and you do gain access, be careful. You'll need to be on your best behavior in private groups, because even gentle sales pitches can be filtered or get you blocked.

Video, Video, Video

Over 50% of Facebook users access it only on a mobile device. There's a ton of video on Facebook, partly a side effect of Facebook trying to clone the YouTube experience. If you're a marketer putting video onto Facebook (and you should be), make sure all your metadata is complete, including good titles and descriptions.

Facebook Messenger Bots

Whenever you use a messaging application, you're probably used to getting a response from a human. A Facebook Messenger Bot is an app for your Facebook page (usually a consumer brand) to provide automated responses to human inquiries. It's like replacing a human customer service rep with a computer. The bot runs within the Messenger app. When a bot is built well, it delivers automated responses that mimic a live person. For example, the 1-800-Flowers chatbot helps the user order flowers via an interactive conversation (see an actual bot session below.)

In China, messaging apps are replacing web browsing. The bots are just automation of the work required to staff the messaging apps. It doesn't look like Facebook bots are going to be adopted in the U.S. at the same level, especially if the public perceives that Facebook is trying to manipulate them, or that the bot is "creepy."

The best way to think about a bot is as an intelligent answering machine for your Facebook page's Messenger account. A Facebook bot fires up when someone opens Messenger from a mobile device. There's no way to promote it, it's just part of your Facebook account, and that's by design. Facebook wants to discourage spammy bots.

If a company wants to promote their bot, for example, by posting a message on a blog saying

"Hey! Check out our bot!" it will get almost no traffic because brand page organic reach. The company would have to run paid ads to get any traffic to the blog post.

Another promotion strategy: run an ad on mobile with the message: "Go to our page and ask us about X." The initial investment is a few hours of labor, or you can grab some templates (see Chatfuel in the next section). At this point, you may think "Gee, it's much easier to give someone a coupon for our web site than to play 100 Questions on Messenger." You'd be right, and that's probably why bots haven't been a runaway success.

How do you add a bot to Facebook?

It's an add-on to your Facebook page, but you'll install it into Messenger. A developer can create your bot (see https://developers.facebook.com/quickstarts). Or to create a bot without any code, Chatfuel seems to be king of the hill. They have a pro package that starts at $15 per month. https://chatfuel.com/

Despite the lack of free promotional opportunities, you can't beat the instant gratification or the "cool" factor of an immediate bot response. Check out these screenshots of Kayak, 1-800-Flowers, and Taco Bell bots in action:

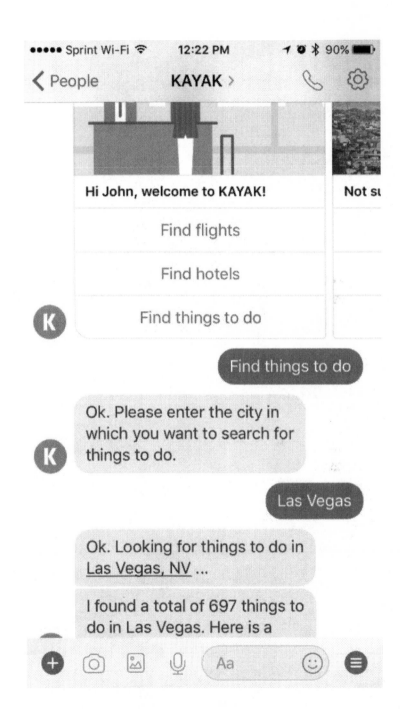

< People   **KAYAK** >   📞   ⚙️

Hi John, welcome to KAYAK!   Not su

Find flights

Find hotels

K   Find things to do

Find things to do

K   Ok. Please enter the city in which you want to search for things to do.

Las Vegas

Ok. Looking for things to do in <u>Las Vegas, NV</u> ...

I found a total of 697 things to do in Las Vegas. Here is a

➕   📷   🖼️   🎤   (Aa   ☺)   ☰

Get Started

Welcome to the 1-800-Flowers Assistant! 🌷

You can easily shop our selection of truly original flowers & gifts, track your order, contact our Customer Care team, or check out our FAQs.

 What would you like to do today? 👻

Buy a gift!

 Let's get started! Select from one of our curated collections:

Send a Message...

Start Over

Facebook Live Video

Not only is Facebook Live challenging Snapchat with filters, they now have a live API. This is a big deal for anyone who doesn't want to look like an amateur using a mobile phone to broadcast video for a brand.

Third party cameras can transmit their video into the live API. For example, you could showcase an on-stage, live video stream from a DJI drone (a flying camera) into Facebook Live. The API has opened up so you're not confined to phone cameras, which have come a long way in quality, but are still not as good as a professional point-and-shoot camera.

Live video on Facebook is a no-brainer if:

- Your organization routinely runs events

- You have a dynamic CEO who speaks at events

- You have a way to leverage and promote live video on Facebook

All it takes to create a professional broadcast is a good switcher board (like one of the old Avid boards) and multiple cameras. But be advised: As of August 2018, you need to be an approved partner to use Facebook Live (it's a dangerous tool in the wrong hands):

https://developers.facebook.com/docs/videos/live-video/

Facebook 360

Facebook is "all in" with the concept of providing viewers with an immersive experience. If you load a panoramic photo into Facebook, it will auto convert to a 360° photo. Almost any cell phone can take a panoramic photo, so get on the FB immersive view train now. A 360° video requires a camera with multiple lenses; it's an emerging technology and we can't recommend one unless you are comfortable doing software updates or throwing cash at a camera that might be discontinued in less than a couple years. The hardware is just not ready for the mass market… yet.

Here's a 360° view of John wearing a T-Shirt, in December, at Bonnie Lee Farm in Williamstown, MA http://bit.ly/2AMRDCS

More about Facebook 360: https://facebook360.fb.com/

Facebook Marketing Hack

Here's a hat tip to Jon Loomer (www.JonLoomer.com) for this cool Facebook targeting and retargeting option. You can target people for retargeting ads who've been to your web site multiple times. For example, you can target the top 10% of the most frequent visitors, and show them different ads than the bottom 90%. But keep in mind that you'd do this only if you had a person whose whole job is managing Facebook ads, because it takes a lot of integration or a lot of list loading to perform correctly. But agencies do see a huge ROI on this type of segmentation. In B2B marketing, you can use this segmentation to provide custom content based on position in the sales funnel: prospects get white papers and webinars, engaged leads are offered video testimonials.

Twitter

Twitter Character Limit

Twitter increased its character limit for tweets to up to 280 characters in November 2017.

Chris performed a study while at Shift Communications on the effect of Twitter's increase in their character limit that took effect in November 2017. He found that some big brands and politicians do go as high as the 280 character limit, but overall, the general public has been trained to stick to the 140 character limit. The primary net effect of the higher limit is to make writing tweets easier for people who would have been stuck at 140 characters, so that little to no editing needed to write a typical tweet.

Chris's Twitter Insurance Experiment

Twitter's future was in question at one time in the past. So Chris put on his martech opportunist hat to save his Twitter followers from extinction. He sent out an automated direct message campaign slowly to his Twitter followers; the campaign was scrubbed against his current newsletter list, and sent out very slowly. The DMs said 'hey, in case Twitter's future is not as bright as we all want it to be, please connect with me on these other services.' The campaign was hugely successful, resulting in more newsletter subscribers and LinkedIn connections.

LinkedIn connections are doubly useful, not just for the networking juice, but also because LinkedIn has a robust data export, i.e. an efficient way of capturing your social networking audience. (If you're not following Chris on

Twitter yet, we recommend that you start. You'll see first-hand how he markets on Twitter, encourages newsletter signup from Twitter, etc.)

How Does Twitter Beat Facebook?

Chris: "I would like to see Twitter thrive, because for us as marketers, every single social media monitoring tool is vastly overweight on Twitter data, especially influencer identification. The other social media networks don't have the same open flow of information. You can see some content on Facebook pages that are public, but you can't see personal posts. You can see Instagram posts, but there's no clickable links in them; only ads contain clickable links. You can see Pinterest pins that are public, but not pins on private or friend boards. That lack of transparency means there's a lot of dark social media. Twitter is the last bastion of non-dark social."

John: "While it's true that bots keep pumping garbage on Twitter, they've been reined in. Now bots have to behave more like humans - a minimum of 2 minutes between tweets, no more than 10 tweets/hour, and other restrictions. Between throttling and better detection of fake accounts, bots are less of a problem. Twitter is still best for ease of getting data and following links."

LinkedIn

LinkedIn Hack for Job Hunters

Chris: "If you've ever logged into LinkedIn, one of the first things you'll see at the top of your page are those people who've viewed your profile. If you click on that, you'll see the last five people who viewed it. To see more of the people who checked you out, you need to upgrade.

Here's how to flip that around if you're a job hunter. Let's say you're job hunting for a marketing position in the Greater Boston Area. Type into Google:

site:linkedin.com/in "Greater Boston" "VP Marketing"

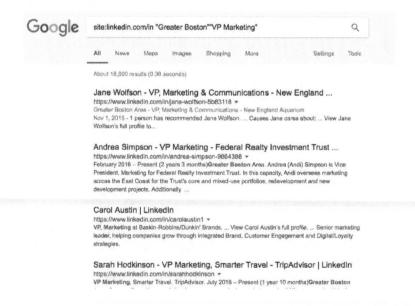

That query will display everyone in LinkedIn in the Greater Boston area with VP of Marketing in their LinkedIn profiles.

You can then log into LinkedIn (open multiple tabs), and click on the result generated from Google. When you click on those VP of Marketing profiles, you'll show up in those accounts as someone who's viewed their profile. It's an easy, free way to get some visibility with prospective employers. To get the "billboard effect" when your profile is displayed by any VP Marketing that checks out your profile, make sure the top of your profile shows a short snippet of your skills. If you're unemployed, say that you're looking for a new opportunity right up front.

Note: Salespeople, DO NOT abuse this technique. John and Chris already hate LinkedIn requests where the person's individual profiles is 'do you need a website for $295?'"

John: "All ham. No spam. That's our motto on LinkedIn."

Open Candidates Function

You can reach out to recruiters and put yourself on the job market without it being publicly announced on LinkedIn. LinkedIn's blog gives you step-by-step instructions here: http://bit.ly/2w0q8kc

Use Discretion

LinkedIn is a great tool, and you can't beat it for B2B social media. But we recommend that you don't accept all invitations. You want to link to the people you know and trust, otherwise you run the risk of getting served all kinds of promotional garbage.

Videos Rule

Chris: "Loading videos onto LinkedIn has been off-the-rails good. I posted a video about the basics of marketing automation, and that video got almost 30,000 views within about a week. The same video on YouTube was viewed only 30 times. The high viewership is mostly likely due spot-on business content (tailor-made for LinkedIn), and also probably my high number of first-degree business connections (which may be a factor in LinkedIn's content-scoring algorithm.)"

Pinterest

Audience Targeting

Pinterest has picked up momentum on the advertising front, and seems to be on parity with the rest of the social network platforms now.

Pinterest offers:

- Customer Targeting (upload your customers)

- Act-a-like Targeting (behavioral)

- Visitor Targeting (more commonly known as Retargeting; Google calls it Remarketing)

Info on marketing on Pinterest here: https://business.pinterest.com/en/pinterest-audience-targeting

If you're doing any kind of influencer analysis on visual content, Pinterest is one of the best places to go. Their ads seem to be on par with Instagram's ads. So if you've got an

Instagram ad strategy, you should be able to pick it up and plop it over onto Pinterest.

Good MarketingLand article on Pinterest Ad Targeting here: https://mklnd.com/2KRzfsS

Snapchat

A Business Case for Snapchat?

Shift Communications did a Google survey of consumers who are 18+ years old and frequent Snapchat users.

They asked questions like:

"Do you follow any brands?

"Have you bought anything from a brand?"

"Have you considered buying from any brands whose Snapchat content you've seen?"

"Do you recommend a brand's Snapchat channel to anyone?"

Most people said "Nope!"

Based on that data (admittedly, a little old at the time of publication), there doesn't appear to be a business case for SnapChat. So far, there's no analytics, no business KPI, the ads are relatively expensive, and very little data about performance is provided. Experiment with Snapchat if your target is 12 - 24 year-old consumers.

Chapter 3: How to Use Google Tools

The upshot of this chapter, and our one, overarching piece of advice: Use Google Tools. The great news is that almost all of them are free. Until Google is displaced, you are best served by worshipping its tools. Google continues to expand its capabilities, the majority of which are truly useful to marketers.

However, we find that a good number of marketers don't even have the basics maximized, such as installing Google Analytics (and more importantly, putting in the work to learn how to set it up correctly so that attribution is correct and all the results aren't just in a huge data pile under AdWords).

This chapter serves a decent checklist of both intro and intermediate tactics to help you figure out if you're using Google to its fullest.

Google Analytics
> **User Explorer**
> **How to Use GA to Calculate Complex Sale Goal Value**
> **How To Check Every Page For GA & Tag Manager Tags**
> > **Google Analytics Suite - Google Optimize**
> > **The Quadrant Review: Web Site Productivity**
> > **GA Skewing Referral Source**

Google Tag Manager (GTM)
> **Google Tag Management**
> **Google AutoTrack v. Google Tag Manager**

Google Data Studio
> **Why and How to Build Your Dashboard**
> **The Power of Self-Service**

Google Accelerated Mobile Pages (AMP)

Google Analytics

User Explorer

We think User Explorer is a very powerful tool, allowing users to drill down to the individual paths through your website. This info on individual behavior can help you identify successful user pathways, as well as places where people get bogged down. You can't reverse engineer to see exactly who's doing what, but you can get a great view of your sales funnel if you include your e-commerce system in your Google Analytics; you'll get a good sense of which pages are most popular or on the critical path to purchasing.

Because users are cookied, you cannot trace back to see exactly who the user is, but you can get basic info such as:

- Device used

- Product pathway: How the individual enters the site, views the product, purchases it

- Sessions

- Average session duration

- Goal conversion rate

- Transactions and other metrics

67

Below is screenshot from Marketing Over Coffee's Google Analytics, tracking the performance of one person during a single session:

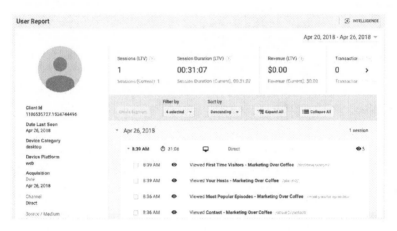

To better see Google Analytics in action, you can watch Chris's demo here: http://bit.ly/2P4790Z

Here's a fact that doesn't get discussed much, but it's critical. Each web visitor who gets tracked in your analytics is assigned a Google ID, so you can tell when individuals make a return visit. There's a similar ID for app users on mobile devices. Google Analytics can match these two IDs, so that you can now track individuals across both their desktop or phone. For example, when you look up a product on Amazon from your computer, you may start to get retargeting ads for those products on the Facebook app on your phone.

The User Explorer info can also help with developing unique landing pages; if there's a fixed group of people that only gets access to a certain entry point (for example, a landing page for club members), you could filter on that and have a better group to watch.

At a minimum, you need to understand these traffic and purchasing patterns:

- Who spends the most time (i.e. highest number of sessions) on your website

- What's the behavioral pattern of your most frequent users

- Which behavioral patterns generate the highest revenue/highest number of leads

These slices of your audience will give you insights that you can use to improve the transaction experience and your site overall.

How to Use GA to Calculate Complex Sale Goal Value

Chris: "Setting goals and goal values is one of the most important things you can do with Google Analytics (GA), second only to actually installing it properly." Chris's blog gives you the steps to calculate Net Customer Value (NCV), Net Deal Value (NDV), Sales Lead Qualified Value (SLQV), Marketing Qualified Lead Value (MQLV), and Prospect Value (PV). You should compare how you're using GA metrics v. Chris's metrics: http://bit.ly/2MfDaFt

How To Check Every Page For GA & Tag Manager Tags

If your site's traffic is declining, it may be due to the removal of the Google Analytics tracking code. It's a pretty common problem, due to aging websites, inadvertent removal of coding, etc.

Chris used his software skills to build a great, FREE tool that will crawl your entire website and tell you if you have Google Analytics tags installed on every page. The tool is on his blog:

http://bit.ly/2P70P94

(And if you're not subscribing to his newsletter -- that's another free resource you really add to your arsenal.)

Google Analytics Suite - Google Optimize
https://www.Google.com/analytics/optimize/

There are 2 versions of Google Analytics: the free version (which most of us use) and the paid, Google 360. Google provides a great comparison matrix here: https://www.google.com/analytics/analytics/compare/

Tag Manager has evolved into middleware, and marketers use it to get out from under IT. It used to be that every time you added a tool to your stack, you'd have to ask IT to add some code to your website. Because the code needs to be on every page, the process isn't trivial if you don't know what you're doing. But with Tag Manager, you add the Google code to your website just once, and after that instead of adding code to your site, you add it to your Google Tag Manager account (circumventing your own IT). Just be aware that there are some downsides: There's some lock-in; it can be difficult to get other analytics to work with GTM. There's no support, so you're on your own if you have any problems. With all tag managers, there's some security risk. If someone cracks into it, or there's an exploit, outsiders could inject their code into your site.

With Optimize, you can rewrite your website and do multi-variate testing on any page with Tag Manager installed. For example, Chris ran a test on his personal website: a blue button against a red button on his newsletter pop-up. He also tested a bigger button against a smaller button. Chris is the master of pop-ups -- see them in action here: http://www.christopherspenn.com

Optimize means you don't have to make any changes to the website itself, which is a huge advantage for companies whose marketing departments don't have control of the website. You control all the layout changes in Optimize, and you'll be able to perform statistical testing and optimizing of test variables inside of Tag Manager.

John: "I have an insider trick that involves Optimize also. If you're someone with little time or budget, pull up a competitor that uses Optimize or a similar tool, like Ghostery. Try to identify what you can steal from their landing page v. someone who's not using an optimization tool; that will give you access to some of their tested insights." (P.S. Never assume what works for someone else will work for you; always test new variables.)

Chris: "Optimize ties in deeply with Google Analytics. So if you want to set up an audience in Google Analytics -- for

Web Page Revenue
Maximizer

High	HIGH Page Views LOW $$$ Opportunity: Improve Conversion Actions: Better Calls to Action, Pop-Ups, etc.	HIGH Page Views HIGH $$$ Opportunity: Send More Traffic Actions: Paid & non-paid promotion
Page Views	LOW Page Views LOW $$$ Opportunity: None Actions: N/A	LOW Page Views HIGH $$$ Opportunity: Identify Rising Stars Actions: Send More Traffic: Paid & non-paid promotion, does page revenue/leads go up wit more exposure?
Low	Low	High

$$ Revenue Per Page

example, everyone from LinkedIn -- you can pass that to Optimize and test content changes only for people coming to a web page from LinkedIn. The same applies to Facebook traffic, or traffic from specific ads, etc. You can then pass that info to Adwords; once you know what works for the

LinkedIn audience, you can run display ads to retarget those folks."

The Quadrant Review: Web Site Productivity

One of the easiest ways to improve revenue or leads from your web site is to evaluate pages based on revenue generated, or leads generated v. page views. In Google Analytics, you can set up events (things viewers do), then set up goals (triggered on specific events), and you can put a dollar amount on the goals.

Use the quadrant format below to identify areas of opportunity. HINT: Great project for a marketing intern, or for a newer, lower level marketer to earn their spurs.

GA Skewing Referral Source

If you haven't added your domain to your Google Analytics referral exclusion list yet, you need to fix that oversight ASAP.

The rationale: When you see your own domain as a referral source to your web site in Google Analytics, repeatedly, it's usually due to Google ignoring the original referral source after the 30-minute timeout Google imposes. Google will code the subsequent session (after the timeout) as coming from your website, i.e. a self-referral.

As an example, suppose someone is referred to the Marketing Over Coffee website via a link in a blog. The reader clicks from the blog to the MoC website. Then the reader get distracted, has lunch, leaves for a meeting, but then come back after 30 minutes and resumes browsing the MoC site. The original referral source is the blog. But the second session, which occurs after the 30-minute timeout, is considered a new session by Google, and the referring source is your own website.

To maintain the original referral source for that session after the time-out, you need to add your website domain to your referral exclusion list. This article from Search Engine Land gives you the instructions on how to implement this 5-minute fix: https://selnd.com/2B52Pvs

Google Tag Manager (GTM)

Google Tag Management

Google Tag Manager is critical. It improves your site and makes it work better, so make sure you've got it set up.

There are a lot more enterprise-level capabilities in GTM, especially now that it's part of their paid Google Analytics 360 Suite.

One of the most important functionalities is that Google Tag Management has automatic malware detection. For example, if you put in a tag that's mistakenly carrying malware, Google will auto block it. Google will also let you do staging environments (creating production conditions for testing that are close to the real-world), which are important for quality assurance.

GTM also does a great job of supporting collaboration and teams, instead of being a one-off system more geared to support individual users. It has the functionality that you would expect from an enterprise tool to support functions like version control, control rollbacks, and very granular control.

If you're already heavily invested in the Google ecosystem, you should be using Tag Manager.

Google AutoTrack v. Google Tag Manager

[Warning: This advice is directed to our most technical marketers and their webmasters. If you're not in that venerable group, please feel free to blow past this section.]

Google's AutoTrack is a library that supposedly enables Google Analytics to perform more functions, and is attractive to some for its ability to do some unique, fairly specialized stuff. It's written in Javascript, and there's a developer kit for it. In Google's words: "Autotrack is a developer project intended to demonstrate and streamline some advanced tracking techniques with Google Analytics, and it's primarily intended for a developer audience." Google provides some of the use cases for AutoTrack here: https:// analytics.googleblog.com/2016/08/autotrack-turns-10.html

But GTM is a better overall solution. If you're not using a tag management system, you're just asking for trouble. You're usually better off investing time in GTM instead. Just be sure to test GTM once you've installed it (your webmaster should understand the intricacies and potential pitfalls involved with web services getting data routed through Google instead of your web site.)

The key point: If you're already using GTM to its fullest, Google AutoTrack has some developer tools you can use if GTM is lacking features you need.

This article provides a good review of when it's best to use GA AutoTrack:

https://www.blastam.com/blog/google-analytics-autotrack-should-you-use-it

Google Data Studio

Why and How to Build Your Dashboard

If you haven't used Google Data Studio yet, you're missing a really good opportunity to build clever dashboards that will give you the insights you need. Caution: don't throw any old data onto the dashboard.

You want to strive for a "Why-How" structure to your dashboard. At the top of the dashboard should be the "Why" of the KPIs, such as revenue (it's the big green or red arrow). In the middle, display the trending data about those KPIs. The "How" section are your diagnostic metrics: all of the factors that feed into the KPIs.

If you structure your dashboards with those key metrics front and center, you'll get much more executive acceptance. In other words, "will we make this quarter's numbers?"

Updating your dashboard with Google Data Studio is an effective way to organize your stats, and it doubles as good internal PR. Use it!

The Power of Self-Service

There are two more super helpful layers of the Google stack: Google Sheets and Google BigQuery.

Everyone who is in the Google ecosystem should be using Data Studio. It lets you build nice interactive dashboards from all your Google data. You can store any kind of data such as data from Analytics, AdWords, and YouTube, in a Google Sheet or BigQuery.

You can create "one-stop shopping" dashboards that you can just hand off to your senior execs: "Here's the data on our YouTube and AdWords ads, and our analytics and social media data." Your executives can also self-serve their reporting needs by adjusting timeframes or other variables. If your management is willing to do their own adjustments, it will liberate you from having to provide custom, on-demand reporting.

Data Studio is still in Beta, but they now have over 80 connectors including Twitter, Amazon, and others.

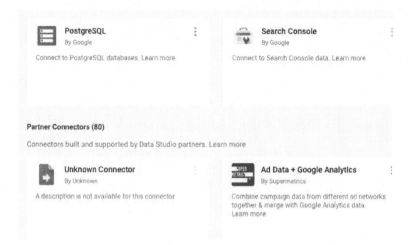

At the time of publication, Google Data Studio has free unlimited reporting (a benefit which was initially reserved for paid Google 360 customers).

Google Accelerated Mobile Pages (AMP)

https://developers.Google.com/AMP/

Putting Mobile First

AMP is Google's recipe for faster, better browsing on the mobile platform. Google gives AMP-optimized pages preference in search listings, if it's a mobile-ready app. If you make your website AMP-ready, it will serve up a small, slimmed-down page.

AMP works for big and small businesses. If you're using WordPress, the plug-in is free. Just do exactly what Google says to do. If you have a CMS, check with the vendor about how to implement it. But you'll want that cost-free, extra traffic.

Chris discovered that AMP definitely increased his web site traffic; Google AMP pages increased from 0% to 4% of Chris's website traffic. He also saw a similar increase in client analytics. The web site traffic appears to be net new traffic from mobile via organic search, i.e. incremental traffic, no cannibalization from existing desktop traffic.

Here's a link so you can see how the carousel of results looks on a mobile device.

https://googleblog.blogspot.com/2015/10/introducing-accelerated-mobile-pages.html

Great Moz article about Mobile-First Indexing: https://moz.com/blog/amp-digital-marketing-2018

SEO

Prepping for the "New SEO"

While being findable is the still the core of SEO, the "how" of SEO is changing. Now that Google is using AI to rank, techniques such as keywords, exact match domains, and header tags are less important (although you still need to invest in classic SEO techniques before going hog wild with AI).

We know that Google uses AI to rank based on semantics. It also uses AI to curate topics and concepts, and then uses natural language processing to match to topics and concepts.

To optimize your organic search results, you're going to need expertise in machine learning, artificial intelligence, and neural networks to optimize your organic search results. John expects various vendors like ahrefs, Moz, SEMRush, SpyFu and similar companies to adapt.

Examine your pages from a topic and cluster perspective. Identify the top 10 results for your preferred search terms, then use the AI tools (topics and cluster) to reverse engineer what Google sees. Keep in mind that Google has the cloud natural language processing, so you can use their own technology to determine what Google thinks the top 10 results have in common.

That answer reveals how to build your own content.

For big brands, you'll need expertise in machine learning, AI, and neural networks to achieve optimal SEO. You can get a jumpstart by building against the AI algorithms that are available to developers: scrape all those top 10 pages and feed them into your AI learning algorithm. The AI will then spit back what the top scorers have in common. The results will help you nail language, phrases to include in your content. (It's also a stealth method of finding out all the insider lingo.)

But both small brands and large brands need to keep in mind that Google results are still a black box. Getting the right phrases may be only 10% of why things rank. For example, using keywords and phrases is an independent factor from the positive ranking effect of getting a large volume of referring traffic from other sites.

Keep in mind that the race is to the swift in the case of AI-aided organic search. John expects that SEO tools will offer this capability within a couple of years. And once everyone is using the same tools, the competitive advantage will decrease.

Chris breaks it down on his blog: http://bit.ly/2nAaF6D

Pop-ups + Mobile Devices = Lower Google Rank

Google dropped the hammer on mobile sites that include pop-ups around January 2017. In Google's words: A "technique that makes content less accessible to a user: showing a popup that covers the main content, either immediately after the user navigates to a page from the search results, or while they are looking through the page."

To keep Google from decreasing your ranking (and consequently, the traffic sent to your site), you need to make sure that your plug-in manufacturers have made their mobile pop-ups compliant with Google's requirements. Google might be ok with a non-intrusive lower third style pop-up on a mobile device, but a full-page pop-up is not OK.

If you've got software that you use from a developer, hold them accountable for meeting Google's requirements. Ask for a deadline by which the software and/or plug-ins you use are going to be converted, or let the developer know you'll be switching to a compliant vendor.

More info on how Google uses ease of content accessibility from mobile devices as a factor in ranking: http://bit.ly/ 2BjIpiH

Chapter 4: Artificial Intelligence & Machine Learning

Quick Primer
    Machine Learning v. Artificial Intelligence (AI)
    AI: The Major Players
    Machine Intelligence Vendor Chart
Marketing and AI
    What Marketers Can Do Now
    Marketing Analytics AI Framework
    The New SEO is Machine Learning
    Natural Language Interpretation: The
Screenless Revolution
    What Watson Can Do For Marketers
    Watson Analytics
    Watson Digital Marketing
    Watson Analytics for Social Media
    Watson Visual Recognition
    MoC What-If: Can John Retire?
    Chris' AI Press Release Experiment
    Marketers Need Technologists
Cool and Practical Stuff AI Can Do Now
    Google Translate
    AI Milestone: KITT vs. Terminator
    Donut-Free Cops
    AI: 1, Medical Doctors: 0
    Site-Based Marketing
    Baseball
    Audition
    Cardiac Monitoring
AI Is Far From Perfect
AI Is Far From Safe
The Human Cost
    CMOs Are Not Ready

AI and Marketing Jobs Long-Term
Beyond Marketing: Looking at the Larger Economy
AI for President?

Quick Primer

When it comes to AI, Chris is convinced that the Terminators are on their way and that most of us will end up slaving away for the machines. John is more optimistic, and thinks that the machines will make humans better - more KITT than Terminator.

But in terms of the more immediate future, Marketing Over Coffee has been lucky to have access Chris's knowledge and work in AI, especially his marketing-related AI experiments. If you're not planning to get down into the muck of AI, you owe it to yourself to check out Chris's company: Trust Insights https://trustinsights.ai

But whether you're going to invest in AI directly, or hire out AI research, you can get a good overview from our "best of AI" from past MoC podcasts.

Machine Learning v. Artificial Intelligence (AI)

Machine Learning is exactly how it sounds. A machine or an algorithm has the ability to learn by itself, to make iterative changes to things.

An example of machine learning: In Excel, type in the number "1." The next cell down, type in the number "2." If you highlight the first two cells, and drag the cursor to the next cell down, Excel will automatically see the pattern (prior value +1), and the cell will fill with the number 3.

Machine Learning isn't Artificial intelligence (AI) because it is based on an algorithm; nothing new has been created. Machine learning is a subset of AI. Marketers have been using machine learning for more than a decade, generally built into software tools, such as Google Analytics, Excel and Buffer.

Artificial Intelligence is defined as a machine that can learn on its own and create something new. The creation may be based on pre-existing knowledge, i.e. a blog post is built from letters and words, but the end result is not a mere extension of the inputs --- the end result is new and different from the inputs.

AI applies to Marketing in the form of Natural Language Processing with IBM's Watson as one of the best examples. For example, NLP provides the ability to take a piece of unstructured online text or a blog post, and based on algorithms, be able to read like a human and discern the nature and meaning of the content. Why is this AI valuable? There's no limit to the reading capability of AI (unlike humans, or even distributed human systems, with built-in limits of time and attention).

In addition to being able to read content, AI can differentiate between the type of information published, and the "tone" and personality of the content. That automated discernment can be interpreted into data that can be classified and managed.

One interesting area is AI's ability to "detect" personality. AI can take a piece of text, and based on what the AI knows about human personality and psychology, it can "fingerprint" the author. The AI can even isolate and describe the characteristics of the author's writing style.

AI: The Major Players

The big platforms are:

- Amazon Machine Learning

- Google Cloud Machine Learning Engine

- IBM Watson

- Microsoft Azure ML

- Python

- TensorFlow

The 4 best-known providers of AI tools: Amazon, Facebook, Google and IBM (that's in addition to the huge amount of AI tools built via open source).

Each company's approach to AI, and consequently, the algorithms developed by each company, have evolved from their core business and information infrastructure.

Chris notes: "Marketing doesn't have a reputation for being technologically well-developed, so there's significant potential to use AI. You may have a lot of data, and want to apply machine learning to it, but the difficulty is getting started. Your best strategy is to pick a platform you can afford, and that you're good at using (or you think you can develop the necessary proficiency.)

To pick the right AI, you need to figure out what kind of problem you're trying to solve, and then pick the corresponding solution."

- Amazon - Super predictive in terms of product purchasing. They have a lot of machine learning capabilities, but is not as robust in AI capabilities.

- Facebook - conversation expertise. Their AI is focused on how to have conversations with humans.

- Google -- a search-and-find expertise

- IBM [Watson]-- Based on cognition and "fuzzy" systems, leading to the ability to try and behave like a human.

Tech Note: Most of the AIs have an open sourcing to portions of their software. For example, you can get under the hood and see how Google thinks about AI by dissecting TensorFlow, an open source machine learning framework.

If you want to get started with AI, look at IBM Watson, Google's cloud platform, and Amazon Web Services. There's an enormous amount of opportunity for savvy, interested marketers, especially marketing technologists.

Machine Intelligence Vendor Chart

John realizes that there's been a lot of vendor turnover since this chart was originally published, but he thinks that it's still the best landscape of AI companies available: https://oreil.ly/2OzJfcM

Also, beware of shameless trendjacking: Because AI is too hot a topic to ignore, be aware of vendors who are, all of a sudden, AI companies.

Marketing and AI

What Marketers Can Do Now

The early AI wins for marketers is going to come from their access to a goldmine of marketing data, including Google Analytics, 22+ years of purchase data, 10 years of social data, and other data.

We can upload all this marketing data into an AI and have it:

- Learn from the data

- Identify any trends or outliers

- Make recommendations for future action (predictive analytics)

Let's look at a "blue sky" example: What if the AI found there's a significant relationship between StumbleUpon forwards and the bounce rate on e-commerce web pages when the item is colored blue? That's the kind of seemingly illogical, deep-digging algorithms that AI can detect.

A very preliminary way to use AI is to ask it to do something an intern can do, because an AI's capabilities for learning is, at a minimum, similar to that of an intern. For example, you wouldn't ask an intern to rebalance your organization's finances, but you can use an AI's exploratory capabilities to dig into your financial data --- assuming that your organization's financial data is correct.

Marketing Analytics AI Framework

Bots are being developed as a customer-facing capability. But marketers are going to first experience AI on the analytics side.

Model: The 5-Level Hierarchy of AI for Marketing Analytics

Level 1: Descriptive Analytics

Humans feed the AI with good and accurate raw data. Most organizations are still at this stage. It's not easy to get accurate data.

Level 2: Diagnostic

If you've accomplished Level 1 and your data is accurate, diagnostic AI answers the question "what happened?"

Level 3: Predictive Analytics (Machine Learning)

Based on what's happened in the past (Level 2) what could happen, and what's likely to happen? Systems like Watson are starting to get into this territory, but it's not ready for prime time yet.

Level 4: Prescriptive Analytics (True AI)

After the AI's determined what could happened, Prescriptive Analytics says "Here's the pattern we see, and here's what you should do next." Not ready for prime time yet.

Level 5: Proactive Analytics

Think of this as the self-driving car of marketing: you plug in the system and it does your marketing for you. The machine will execute, and humans are not involved other than to supervise. Does not exist yet.

The New SEO is Machine Learning

Chris: "You should put your content, AND your competitors' content, into these machine learning tools, so you can see what the search engines see when it comes to content and SEO. Because if you don't, you are at the mercy of algorithms that are hard to understand.

The good news is that a lot of this stuff is super cheap. You can deploy Tensorflow (an open source machine learning framework) on your laptop. When you're ready to upgrade, just use a Google Cloud service.

More info on Chris's blog: http://bit.ly/2OBExLD

Natural Language Interpretation: The Screenless Revolution

Chris: "Because people are starting to use voice query devices at home and in the office, marketers have a new challenge: screenless marketing. Due to the voice interface, if you're not

#1 in search results, you are zero; no one's going to stick around to hear the second position results."

Chris advises: "You need to think about how your content can be findable in natural language formats. That means you need to map out your content conversationally, and figure out how your content can be found in natural language, the way a human would actually say something.

For example, let's say you're looking for a marketing podcast. You might type "marketing podcast" into a search engine. But it's more likely that someone would ask Alexa: "Alexa, what's a good marketing podcast?"

There's 3 choices for this technology (automatic speech recognition and natural language interpretation): the IBM universe, the Google universe, and the Amazon universe.

Lex is the most important of Amazon's AI services. It powers Alexa Service via the Amazon Echo, and has automatic speech recognition and natural language interpretation. All these services are available to the general public as APIs. (Check out this page for a good diagram of Lex in action, as well as the massive list of services Amazon provides: https://aws.amazon.com/lex/?nc2=h_a1)

Lex is just one of Amazon's Machine Learning Services. If you don't already have an Amazon Web Services (AWS) account, sign up for an account. (AWS is everything Amazon offers as cloud-based IT services.) There's no cost upfront, and it's currently a pay-as-you-go system.

(https://aws.amazon.com/pricing/?nc2=h_ql_pr&awsm=ql-3)

As for the relationship between search engines and devices: Apple/Siri and Google Home use Google, and Amazon Alexa seems to be using a hybrid, so you need to do optimize for conversation across all the search engines.

Advice and other tips on how to navigate the screenless revolution from Chris's blog:

http://bit.ly/2P5ldr2

What Watson Can Do For Marketers

Chris has experimented extensively with IBM's Watson AI. As he says: "I am a terrible coder but I've been able to get more of Watson to work for me than any of the other systems."

Getting started in AI is easy, regardless of your industry. Watson provides online videos to give you a sense of what's available. You can try each for free, using very limited data sets, but you'll be able to see what's possible, and then start to strategize how to leverage AI for your organization:

Watson Personality Insights: https://www.ibm.com/watson/services/personality-insights/

Watson Discovery: https://www.ibm.com/watson/services/discovery/

Watson Tone Analyzer: https://www.ibm.com/watson/services/tone-analyzer/

Watson Analytics

(Watson Analytics is no longer available for purchase , but IBM has introduced IBM Cognos Analytics 11.1) You can load your data into Watson analytics to perform sophisticated math, such as automated predictive analytics and data discovery. Check out this quick video:

https://www.ibm.com/watson-analytics

Watson Digital Marketing

https://www.ibm.com/customer-engagement/digital-marketing

Watson Analytics for Social Media

This AI can look at the social media landscape for a given topic or set of themes, and provide useful insights. If you have tons of social media data, it can be difficult to identify where you should focus your attention. Watson does a very good job of isolating anomalies worthy of scrutiny.

https://www.ibm.com/products/watson-analytics-for-social-media

Watson Visual Recognition

Watson has been trained to recognize images of common items, like microphones and pizza. Chris experimented with feeding Watson with images from Instagram (not the text, just images), and Watson was able to spit out images in specific categories, like high-rise buildings. It cost Chris 3¢ to scan 10K Instagram posts. (No, that's not a typo.)

How is visual recognition AI useful to marketers? Let's suppose you want to identify the top 10 images on Instagram for a certain period. Or photos of a specific car model. There's no way a human team can do that economically, but Watson can identify those for you. Watson can be trained to recognize images like logos and faces. For example, that variations of a logo can be fed into Watson, so that Watson is trained to recognize the logo, and then Watson can find the top 10K Instagram posts with images containing that logo. It's a whole new level of intelligent listening, especially with AI's ability to react in real-time.

Watson's Visual Recognition Services: https:// www.ibm.com/watson/services/visual-recognition/

MoC What-If: Can John Retire?

Chris envisions an AI-driven scenario that could liberate John from the weekly MoC podcast (although John would probably miss the give-and-take with some of the most interesting and accomplished minds in marketing.)

Chris: "Let's say that Marketing Over Coffee is looking for a blogger. MoC could use AI to fingerprint current blogs to find a blogger whose style is closest to the MoC brand personality. It's also very likely that the audience of any blogger that AI finds is similar to MoC's, because the respective audiences are accustomed to the same voice and subject matter."

Watson's cognitive search engine could also, theoretically, be applied to MoC content creation. Chris riffed on how Watson's Retrieve and Rank AI could create Marketing Over Coffee podcasts:

1. Transcribe every episode of Marketing Over Coffee using Watson

2. Build a collection of marketing questions.

3. Feed the questions, along with the answers from the episodes, into Watson's Retrieve and Rank service.

4. Watson creates a cognitive search engine. For example, let's say that one of the questions is "How can I learn more about ROI?" Watson would identify the top episodes for ROI, but not based on keywords. Identification would based on Watson's actual cognition of the term ROI, and the context in which it's discussed.

Note: These steps are oversimplified, as it downplays the thousands of hours of labor required to train the AI to transcribe the episodes correctly. John is probably on the hook for MoC content for the foreseeable future.

Chris' AI Press Release Experiment

Chris decided to put AI to the test for what should be a very doable, common marketing/PR task: press release generation.

Chris: "I played around with setting up an actual artificial intelligence system on an office-based cloud server with the goal of the AI-generated press releases. I fed the AI with approximately 8,100 press releases, so the AI could learn what's in a press release and then generate its own.

"I found that the process does work. However, there is still the need for a human being in the process. The AI came up not only with some fairly amusing press releases, but also some disastrous screw-ups. There is no way I would ever let the software create and distribute press releases without human oversight."

Marketers Need Technologists

To take advantage of the new AI-related opportunities, and to defend against AI-related competition, marketers need access to marketing technologists or data scientists.

You want to start experimenting with AI now, so that you're not left behind.

It's relatively easy and cheap to get started, but you must have access to development talent and coders. There is currently no plug-and-play, graphical-only, or drag-and-drop AI. You need to have a working knowledge of Python. You should also have database experience: SQL for huge datasets and cloud-based databases like Hadoop and Mongo.

As Chris likes to say, you don't need extreme technical sophistication to get started in AI. For example, if you want to analyze what people saying on social media about Coffee Labeling Laws, go into your social media monitoring system, extract everything people have said, and put it in a database. Then tell the AI to think about it in a defined way, and perform a specific type analysis.

For Chris, that's 20 lines of code, 15 +/-libraries, and a database. In the grand scheme of things, that's not heavy tech lifting. AI will return an array of data to slice and dice, so you can either put it back into a database or put it into visualization software.

Chris performed this analysis on his own Twitter account. The question was: "What are the topics of my most popular tweets?" He extracted all his Twitter data, did some preliminary segmentation by identifying the top 20% of tweets (based on retweet activity), and fed that into an AI. The system produced an array, which he put into visualization software. Armed with this info, he now knows which topics will produce the most retweets. He discovered that food posts are popular on Friday; people like something a little lighter going into the weekend.

Cool and Practical Stuff AI Can Do Now

Chris: "When Watson won Jeopardy 5 years ago, it could perform a 100-calculation computation 1 million times/second. That's 100 x 1 million. Today, it can perform a 1 million-calculation computation 1 million times/second, so it's increased its power on beyond reach.

"When a human makes a mistake, we learn from our mistake. But humans do not and cannot learn perfectly, and we don't share data as a hive mind. To share what we've learned, we could post it on an intranet, on a blog, even write a book. So typically, with some notable exceptions (e.g. Albert Einstein's special-relativity equation $E=mc^2$), human learning is relatively undispersed.

"When Watson makes a mistake and learns from it, all of Watson gets smarter. This continuous, permanent learning is true of all AIs, such as Google's DeepMind.

"AI becomes the smartest doctor in the world, the smartest taxi driver, the smartest bus driver, the smartest everything. Every opportunity that AI has to learn, it learns perfectly."

Humans will never be able to keep up with AI, and what's possible now is amazing. Check out these examples of AI practicality and ingenuity:

Google Translate

There's AI that we can access now for everyday activities. Google's Translate app uses AI to translate text: just hold up your camera to text and the AI can recognize and translate the text in real-time. There are even some headsets that can translate spoken language, again, in real-time: https://tcrn.ch/2B9dO73

AI Milestone: KITT vs. Terminator

John: "I am by no means an expert in the game GO, but it requires far greater skill range than chess. Chess has a narrow band of skill: beginner to expert, but because GO involves a high level of complexity, players have a wider level of expertise."

A computer player can now beat a human GO player. We're moving closer to the Turing Test: machines that can outwit humans.

More info on MarketingLand: https://mklnd.com/2Azi1Rg

Donut-Free Cops

We've started to blend AIs with objects in the physical world. Watch this Dubai-based law enforcement droid in action, including flirting and taking a selfie with a passerby in this video: https://www.youtube.com/watch?v=cMtMk21FZUM

AI: 1, Medical Doctors: 0

This case study proves that Watson is faster more scalable than it's ever been.

From a conference Chris attended: " A woman in Tokyo was diagnosed with specific type of leukemia and she wasn't getting better.

Watson sequenced her genome, and then compared it to info from 200K medical journals. Watson did the entire process (genome sequencing and journal search) in only 10 minutes. Watson determined that the woman had a different kind of leukemia than what the doctors had diagnosed. They changed her treatment and she made a full recovery."

Site-Based Marketing

Molson, the Canadian brewing company, set up a machine in Toronto that would give you a freebie if you said "I am Canadian." The catch that you'd have to say it in 6 different languages to get the reward: https://www.youtube.com/watch?v=CfpatqyujM0

Baseball

Machines have been taught how to write reports based on a dataset. It took a year of iterative work, involving human supervision, but now AI-generated reports are indistinguishable from reports written by humans. Here's an article about how the Associated Press is using AI to generate all the minor league baseball reports: https://tcrn.ch/2MkTC6B

Audition

Audition is an audio editing app that gives you the ability to edit and remix audio the same way you'd use Photoshop for images, and it only costs $20 per month. The current version of Audition can take a training library of your voices, and create a training library synthesis module that can speak in your voice.

Theoretically, if you combine that synthesized voice with Watson and its content creation abilities, in a few years Watson could probably take over podcasts -- maybe even the Marketing Over Coffee podcast. (Interesting concept.)

Adobe Audition: https://www.adobe.com/products/audition.html

Cardiac Monitoring

Chris saw a demo of an embedded cardiac sensor that Watson monitors using its own anomaly detection algorithms. It will notify the doctor if you're having a cardiac event. Here's a Case Study of an Analytics-as-a-Service System for Heart Failure Early Detection: http://www.mdpi.com/1999-5903/8/3/32/htm

AI Is Far From Perfect

Keep in mind anyone who is successful with AI doesn't just "turn it on". They spend months refining it. During the first rounds of training an AI, data hygiene is what's most like to cause inaccurate results. Social media can be filled with a lot of spam and false positives (in this case, a false positive is information that meets your search specifications, but does not pertain to you), and these surprises are at the heart of AI training. CRM systems have fake and dead records, Google Analytics may have structural problems like missing pages, or traffic that should be filtered. A new AI needs to be trained to recognize and filter out "junk" data, and learn how to compensate for missing data.

Sean Zinsmeister: "When a major company like Salesforce endorses a space like AI, you know it's going mainstream. But I encourage people to look at the proven use cases, and the relevancy of those use cases to their business. AI can be a huge help when you get too many leads by prioritizing the leads and better manage the quality of the data, especially at point of entry. AI may also help with personalized email communications, as well as improving the customer journey."

John adds: "With B2C, you have so much data, you can easily see AI generating some returns for you. But with B2B, if you're only selling to about 5,000 people, especially niche solutions, AI may not help much because there's barely any data."

AI imperfection still abounds in verbal recognition: "I asked Siri about the NE Patriots game score and she started playing Barry Manilow's 'Weekend in New England'."

AI Is Far From Safe

If you're a little creeped out about AI, that's understandable. What could go wrong with a corporation having all your financial and personal data, being able to track you everywhere, and having a bunch of cameras and microphones in your home? It's not like data breaches are happening all the time. Oh, wait...

Google has done some interesting work with AIs that proves that AIs can think. They created 3 AIs with the goal that of 2 of them would to communicate with each other using encryption. The goal of the 3rd AI was to try to break into the encrypted communication between the other 2 AIs.

The AI communication-duo was able to engineer their own encryption algorithm to keep the third one out. The scary part is that not only did the 2 AIs succeed in their goal, no human knows the encryption algorithm either.

That's proof that machines can think. We're still a long way from either the Jetsons or the Terminator, but it's not as far off as people think.

Article on Engadget: https://engt.co/2KP5zwK

Google also released an academic paper saying that they recognize that they need to put in an "AI kill switch" in case the AI does become self-aware. Google could pull off SkyNet (the artificial intelligence from *The Terminator*) with Tensorflow. This article goes under the hood on the AI learning process, and how corrigibility works, i.e. how does the robot realize that human intervention is required to improve its learning process. It's pretty heady stuff:

http://bit.ly/2KPpUC0

The Human Cost

CMOs Are Not Ready

Chris gave a talk to 20 +/- CMOs on cognitive marketing, and how AI is going to change everything. He said: "I scared the hell out of the room."

The response from the CMOs? "This feels like when we were blindsided by the marketing technology and automation wave. People took a long time to catch up. AI feels like an entirely new train coming down the tracks and nobody has any idea how to deal with it in a strategic fashion. And it's complicated by how quickly the machines can evolve to teach themselves."

John's response: "Yes, and based on what we learned from the MarTech revolution, people are going to completely underestimate what's going to happen."

AI and Marketing Jobs Long-Term

AI is going to change a lot of marketers' worlds. Think about the huge amounts of time marketers spend writing reports, creating PowerPoints and doing presentations.

Imagine a day when tracking, advertising, analytics, web/social and other systems are connected. AI can develop algorithms that not only identify patterns, but also can predict marketing results, compare to the required marketing results, and then automatically execute marketing programs.

We won't need marketers to do repetitive tasks (like changing a PPC bid based on external circumstances, for example changing PPC copy to promote umbrellas when it's raining.) We also won't need marketers for tasks that the machines can perform better than humans. Marketers need to evolve with the machines, and to learn to train and supervise them properly in order to have jobs.

What about creative work? Are those jobs immune from AI? Chris attended a demo of Watson music, where he walked up to a piano keyboard connected to a laptop (connected to Watson), and banged out 8 or 9 notes. The menu chose a musical genre, like Middle Eastern or rap. Watson took those 8 notes and created a 4-½ minute musical work, complete with drums, backing, orchestration. And it sounded great.

The ability to create music from minimal human input demonstrates that AI can now function as a creative mind. Eventually, marketing tasks which require creativity, such as blog posts and email marketing, can be done by AI.

Machines can also respond to emails, scheduling social media posts, take photos, and do it better than us, because the machines can learn our voice. They can also learn and use our technology.

Based on the exponential rate of AI technology progress, Chris predicts that 50-75% of marketing jobs will be eliminated, because so much of what marketers do is partially routine.

(Chris echoes Seth Godin's predictions, see Seth's interview.)

Beyond Marketing: Looking at the Larger Economy

AI can perform any task that's routine. White-collar professions, some of them highly paid, are at risk as well. Watson took the entire financials of a publicly traded company and performed the equivalent of a multi-million dollar audit, identifying all the financial anomalies in 10 seconds.

The question is: What do we do as a society when the machines can consistently generate work that's as good as, or better, than the work generated by humans? Eventually, many jobs won't require a human. A computer can do the work, and in many cases, do it better than a human.

Computers can make music, create art, write fiction and poetry, and drive cars. And long-term, computers are being developed to do manual labor. Boston Dynamics has robots that are starting to be able to perform cognitive tasks. There are robots in the agriculture field now that can prepare soil, plant seeds and harvest crops.

Meet the Agrobot, a machine that may have harvested the strawberries in your grocery store:

https://on.mktw.net/2w6nwBB

Chris: "In an AI, robot-driven society, companies will be more productive with less human labor. The producers of the technology will get most of the economic benefit, and there will be a considerable number of humans who cannot earn a living. We have income inequality now; under a robot-driven economy, there'll be radical income inequality, because the machine owners don't have to pay robots a living wage. Robots just require maintenance. (Robot repair may be a sustainable career.)

"Should we teach everyone to code? No. Coders are on the hit list of jobs that machines can do. A machine can generate repetitive code easily, and can even generate cognitive code. Coding may evolve to a scenario where the value of humans is in systems level thinking: 'How do I help the machine engineer?' That may be one of the few area left where humans can provide value.

"Within 10-20 years, we'll need to evaluate what it means to be human. If we have good leadership and forward thinking, we can achieve a type of Star Trek utopia. If we don't have good leadership, we'll have a Mad Max dystopia. I don't think there's a lot of room between these scenarios."

AI for President?

Chris: "If an AI became president, it would either become a complete idiot very quickly or figure out that all these humans are just a wasted space."

John: "That's always the risk with these AI things. We are the source of the problems, so it'd be easier to clean house."

Chapter 5: Virtual Reality

Getting Started
Coming Soon to an Arcade Near You
VR: Getting Fit and Other Tips
Can VR Outperform Bars or Couch Viewing?
Two Fun, Easy VR Experiences

If you think VR is limited to gamers, think again. The early predictions were for VR to take off in gaming or social apps (3rd life anyone?), but VR has made more inroads in commercial applications like factory inspections, training, curing cancer and space travel.

As Chris mentioned: "You do need to try VR, and devote a little of your budget to do some R&D, because someone in your space is going to come out with a VR-related product or marketing. You want to be 'first on the block' with VR technology if it matches your product and/or culture. At a minimum, you need to understand and experience the technology."

Getting Started

If you have an Android-compatible device, one of the best ways to get started is to download the free Cardboard Camera app from the Google Play store. The app does a terrific job of automatically converting panoramic photo into true VR photos. It's an easy way to dip your toe into the Cardboard Camera landscape of things. Here are some VR photos of the Bonnie Lea Farm: https://www.roninmarketeer.com/2018/07/09/panoramic-photos/

Note: Facebook has a tool installed so you can scroll around, as if you're inside the photo; you won't be able to see that in action on John's blog photo.

VR headsets on the cheap end ($20 or less) don't have the ability to focus. For less than $35, you can get a mount that has 3 different adjustments; even if you wear glasses, you can adjust it. The right VR headset significantly improves your Google Cardboard app experience: https://amzn.to/2JCqYfO

Coming Soon to an Arcade Near You

The VR (virtual reality) train continues to roar down the track. Virtuix, an omni-directional treadmill manufacturer, partnered with a publisher representing *The Exorcist*, so soon you'll be able to visit your local VR arcade and battle a demon for 20-25 minutes (and if you get truly scared, you can even run away.)

More info here: https://www.vrfocus.com/2018/04/run-around-the-exorcist-legion-vr-when-it-comes-to-virtuixs-omni-vr-treadmill/

VR: Getting Fit and Other Tips

Chris: I've seen the Virtuix Omni, a type of virtual treadmill. It was part of early Oculus discussions and it looks cool. There was one version that also combines the Delta Six, a controller for a Playstation and Oculus." Chris likes the idea of being able to play and workout for an hour.

John: "I know a lot of people that had a lot of success with the Wii Balance Board. The idea of the virtual treadmill is huge. Peloton is very successful, and they're just scratching the surface of internet-connected gym equipment."

Can VR Outperform Bars or Couch Viewing?

After a stint of watching some Hockey in VR with Google Cardboard (https://vr.google.com/cardboard/), John weighed in on this debate of VR v. watching sports on the couch or at a bar with some friends: "The challenge is the display. Google Cardboard is not a perfect viewer. It works best for people with average eyesight, i.e. no corrective lenses (about 35% of the population). And you don't get absorbed by the experience, the way you would with Oculus." So extraverts, beware, it's unclear how you can cheer or jeer sports teams with everyone on the couch, if each person is viewing an event via their own VR.

After using Oculus, Chris sang its praises: "If I were a manufacturer of any display, especially a large screen, like a TV, I would be investing heavily in headset development. What you can do with one of these headsets blows away what you get out of even an 80-inch TV."

Two Fun, Easy VR Experiences

If you haven't tried VR yet, John is a fan of the Fox Sports app (https://www.foxsports.com/mobile) which shows you what a sporting event would look like in VR. See more info in the Apps We Like Chapter.

To experience VR in a multitude of settings, check out https://www.with.in/

There's a ton of different VR experiences, including a seat at a filming of Saturday Night Live so you can see what it's like to be at the show.

Chapter 6: Apps We Like

Business Apps
Travel Apps
Home & Recreation
All-Around Useful

Supposedly, mobile apps are "dead." Every report on monthly app additions makes this claim, as users add almost zero new apps. We use the term "apps" broadly; some apps are available for both iOS and Android, while some can be accessed via the desktop.

But just because the gold rush is over doesn't mean that apps are no longer life-changing. We've compiled the apps that live on our phones, which means they have strong business travel warrior and home tech nerd cred. And they're the major reason we don't ever look up from our phones.

Use the app links we've provided just as a starting point. And definitely share any apps you think we've missed: @mktgovercoffee

Business Apps
Marketing Over Coffee

What it does: Access to all MoC episodes

Cost $1.99

https://apple.co/2MdxpYR

From a non-anonymous app review: "Winner of both Pulitzer and Nobel prizes, loved by millions, and adored by children everywhere, buying this app will make you the best you can be." John especially likes the episode download feature; download an episode so you can play it offline. The app provides access to all episodes since the podcast debut in 2007.

John will throw content into the app early so that the biggest MoC fans will get access to content before anyone else. Sometimes there's even bonus content only available via the app.

And did we mention that the app is only $1.99?

Shure Motiv Audio

What it does: Record

Cost: Free

http://www.shure.com

You can control the sensitivity of the microphone and you can monitor it (wear headphones and hear the recording while it's happening). There are a bunch of other features if you use a Shure mic on your phone.

Evernote

What it does: A note taking app, where you can create and share notes

Cost: Basic- Free Basic Version, Premium-$69.99/year

https://evernote.com/

HubSpot CRM

What it does: CRM

Cost: Free

https://www.hubspot.com/products/crm

Chris: "I'm impressed with the HubSpot CRM app. It's a cost-effective CRM option for my company, Trust Insights. It's been a smooth ride. I love the contact tracking; I can run a lot of sales and marketing processes from my phone."

Otter

What it does: Transcription

Cost: Free for 600 minutes, $9.95 monthly for up to 6,000 minutes

https://otter.ai

Chris relies on Otter.ai for transcription. Otter integrates with Google Calendar; if you head into a meeting, Otter will ask you "Do you want to turn the live transcribe on?" Live quality is not the best, because the transcription is 100% dependent on the quality of the sound from the phone's microphone. For the highest quality of transcription, upload clean audio to Otter.

Rev.com

What it does: Transcription, performed by a human

Cost: $1 per minute

https://www.rev.com/

John: "They put out pretty good transcripts. It's not the least expensive option, but you won't get the goofs and some of the meaning-killing errors that you'll get with AI-driven transcription services."

Slack for Business

What it does: Provides workspace for small teams

Cost: Free

https://slack.com/

Slack is like a chatroom for your company. It replaces a lot of the junk email that goes around in businesses, like 'Cake in the cafeteria at 1 pm!' or 'does anyone know where the toner for the printer in room A is?' The phone app is exceptional; it sucks everyone in, and may demand your attention 24/7.

Hootsuite

What it does: Social Media Management

Cost: Free for 30-days

https://hootsuite.com/#

It's great for social media monitoring and posting. You could have months of tweets stacked up and ready to go. I have standing searches for Marketing Over Coffee, my name, EventHero, etc., and I can see it all from one dashboard.

TweetDeck

What it does: Social Media Management

Cost: Free

https://tweetdeck.twitter.com/

TweetDeck performs most of the same functions as Hootsuite. However, it has an additional Activity Stream function: who liked your tweets, who just started following you, and similar info.

Bitly

What it does: Link shortening and tracking

Cost: Bitly Pro- Free, Bitly Enterprise- $995/month

https://bitly.com/

John: "A great app for throwing off links to others when you want to be able to track if they've been clicked." (If you haven't already, read the Bitly interview in this book.)

SparkMail for iOS

What it does: If you're a Mac user with multiple email accounts, this app lets you bring in Google, Outlook, and Office 365 into one desktop app.

Cost: Free, Premium, and Enterprise pricing

https://sparkmailapp.com/

Scheduling: ScheduleOnce and HubSpot

What it does: ScheduleOnce sets up meetings and calls

Cost: 14-day free trial, Basic- $7.50/month, Professional-$15.80/month, Enterprise- $32.50/month

https://www.scheduleonce.com/pricing

John has been using ScheduleOnce to set up con calls and meetings for years. It integrates with a bunch of calendars and tools, including Outlook, Google, iCloud, Salesforce, Zoom, Zapier and others. Instead of emailing back and forth with someone, or creating a Google or Outlook Calendar invite, the software generates an email proposing different time slots with the message "Click on the time slot that works best for you."

What it does: HubSpot offers software for marketing, sales, and customer service

Cost: Free, Starter- $50/month, Basic- $200/month, Professional- $800/month, Enterprise- $2,400/month

http://bit.ly/2nBzE9Z

HubSpot has the same functionality as ScheduleOnce, and integrates with Google, Outlook 365, and of course, HubSpot. If you spend a lot of time in HubSpot working leads, using HubSpot for setting up meetings is better, because it will track the history in the contact record and you can report against it. You can use both apps at the same time, just use the integration that saves you the most work.

Integration Made (Almost) Painless

John is a true believer in both IfThisThenThat and Zapier: "These are both big-league, tactical marketing tools." If two products don't integrate, you can usually use these tools (they're also apps) to build an integration. Best of all? It only takes is a couple of hours of work by a normal mortal (i.e. not a developer) and a relatively low monthly fee.

Zapier

What it does: Connects apps

Cost: Free, Premium- 14-day free trial, $20+/month

https://zapier.com/sign-up

Zapier is known for helping with the integrations of common marketing and sales enterprise systems, like Marketo, Slack, and HubSpot. You can also set up triggers to get emails ("Zaps") when certain actions occur. (An example of a "Zap": a customer pay via PayPal, and Zapier adds the payee's email to a list in MailChimp.) Zapier can generate a one-off email when an action occurs, or to keep you sane, a "digest" email that compiles info re: actions.

John advises: "If you can put a little time into configuring it, Zapier is very effective. It's the Swiss army knife for integrations."

Chris: "I'm a Zapier power user, using it both for my own projects and while I was at Shift Communications. Our marketing automation system and one of our lead cleansing data software solutions are connected to Zapier."

Free account (core features), 14-day free trial premium features:

https://zapier.com/apps/digest/integrations

Zapier's CEO Wade Foster shared a couple of his favorite zaps on the Stack and Flow podcast:

https://stackandflow.io/episodes/wade-foster-zapier/

IfThisThenThat

What it does: Connects apps and devices

Cost: Free

https://apple.co/2w5uTcy

IfThisThenThat (IFTTT) has a huge following. You can do some practical integrations, for example, email someone via MailChimp if they comment on your WordPress blog. For those who like to hack their home, you can do some cool things, like Google Calendar starting up your Roomba Vacuum at noon, or seeing when your dog walker is doing what they are supposed to. This guy was able to launch his Roomba with Alexa:

https://www.youtube.com/watch?v=qtpOvGpATI4

IFTT has a mind-blowing list of 360 partners; you really owe it to yourself to look through the full list here: https://ifttt.com/search/service.

Travel Apps
Yelp

What it does: User reviews of restaurants, retails stores and other organizations with a physical presence.

Cost: Free

https://www.yelp.com/

John: "There's a buried feature in Yelp, called Monocle, that I use for directions. You can stand on a city street, move your phone, and Yelp will display the directions you would walk to get to a restaurant or other destination."

Waze

What it does: A GPS and carpool app

Cost: Free to download

https://www.waze.com

SpotHero

What it does: Find and pre-pay for parking spots

Cost: Free

https://spothero.com/

The best way to think of this app is as a Hotwire for parking spaces. You look up spaces a few days before you need one, and you reserve a space via the app. By using this app, John says his cost for a parking space in Boston has fallen from about $40/day to about $20/day. Sometimes airport parking is available. And because reserving the space is managed on the app, there's no paper hassle. SpotHero has a great FAQ section, so check it out.

OpenTable

What it does: Find restaurants and place reservations

Cost: Free

https://www.opentable.com/

John will often search on Yelp first to find a restaurant but says the big win with Open Table is you can find out how busy a place really is. If you're not willing to wait until 10 pm for a table at a place that's smoking hot. You might give up a star or two in ratings to get a table at 6 pm.

Flight Tracker

What it does: Track Flights

Cost: Free

https://www.flightview.com/flighttracker/

You know the airlines are always going to let you down. Now you can increase your odds of staying a step ahead of them.

Lyft

What it does: Taxi-type service

Cost: Free

https://www.lyft.com/

In the duel between car services, we try to use Lyft because they treat their employees well.

TomTom Go

What it does: Vehicle navigation

Cost: Free, in-app purchases (buy more miles per month)

http://bit.ly/2Mhrxhg

John: "I've definitely geeked out when it comes to extra gear in my car to use the TomTomGo. The Flex has a custom mount form Panavise http://panavise.com I use Bluetooth adapters https://amzn.to/2KOwM3n from Anker in both cars because our cars are so old. I also use an Anker two-port charger: https://amzn.to/2IXuXiE. In the Civic, I gave up a cup holder slot for this: https://amzn.to/2KysUYd (it's better than the Panavise mount.)

Home & Recreation
Slice

What it does: Customized pizza from independently-owned pizzerias

Cost: Free

https://apple.co/2MevGmg

John likes this app because he can order pizza online from his local Mom and Pop pizza joints; they'd have no clue how to set up online ordering, so this app picks up the slack.

Runtastic for Running

What it does: Tracks running and fitness metrics

Cost: Free, has in-app products, a premium version is available

https://www.runtastic.com/

John likes their Heart Rate Monitor integration. He says "I've used it for a couple of years. It's not perfect, but it's the best one out there."

Ski Tracks for Skiing

What it does: Track your skiing stats in an app

Cost: $0.99

https://www.corecoders.com/ski-tracks-app/

Quicken

What it does: Personal Finance

Cost: Starter- $34.99/year, Deluxe- $49.99/year, Premier- $74.99

https://www.quicken.com

John's been using Quicken for almost 20 years now. The key advantage is that it makes all the paper go away. You can also answer these type of questions in an instant: "How much have I been spending on groceries, by month, for the last 10 years?" It's also useful at tax time because it can generate reports by category of spending.

ComiXology

What it does: Digital comics from publishers like Marvel, DC, Image, BOOM, IDW, Top Shelf, and Oni Press

Cost: most range from $.99 - $6.99, plenty of free trial issues and monthly subscription available.

https://www.comixology.com/

John: "You don't have to go to the comic store anymore (if you can find one.) ComiXology sells all the old issues. You can also subscribe and get a ton of comics for a flat rate of $5.99/month. They also have 'Guided View' technology, where it smartly pans around the artwork, giving it a cinematic feel that can't be matched on paper." Full interview with the Co-Founder/CEO here: http://bit.ly/2MqqX03

FoxSports VR

What it does: Watch sports in VR

Cost: Free

https://www.foxsports.com/virtual-reality

If you haven't tried VR yet, John recommends FoxSports VR as a first virtual reality experience. Try one of the many headsets around $30 that have better adjustment and focus options.

Logitech Harmony Universal Remote Control

What it does: Universal Remote Control

Cost: $69.98

John: "You can tell it about all your remotes and it will mimic them all. With one button, it turns on my TV, the audio receiver, the Blu-Ray disk player, and can control the TiVo and cable box. The app that you use to set it up also works as a remote, so now your phone can control all the devices too. It also integrates with Alexa, so I can say 'Alexa, tell Harmony to shut off the TV' when the kids need to be corralled to the dinner table."

https://amzn.to/2IyKHJ6

Nest

What it does: Remote temperature monitoring

Cost: Free, but you need to buy the Nest Thermostat

John has a smart thermostat, so he's been using the Nest app. He says he joined the smart revolution about 5 years late, but at least he's onboard now. The killer feature is the ability to check your house's temperature and change it from anywhere. A must-have if you own a second home and/or rental properties.

Meater

What it does: Bluetooth-Enabled, Wireless Smart Meat Thermometer

https://meater.com/

John: "You'd presume that cooking steaks and nailing them perfectly every time is a big deal. But breakfast sausage is the killer app. Before Meater, I was afraid of contaminated pork, so I cooked it until I was making beef jerky out of my breakfast sausage. Also great for your Thanksgiving turkey. Meater has now saved my steaks twice from grease fires because I'm too lazy to clean my grill."

Chris notes (diplomatically): "Eating a mostly vegetarian diet also helps. You can be sure that your soy burgers aren't at risk for salmonella."

Star Trek Timelines

What it does: Explore the Final Frontier

Cost: Free, in-app purchases

https://apple.co/2KRTy9F

John gives a shout out to John Radoff, Boston-area entrepreneur and creator of this app.

The app is any Trek fans' greatest dream come to life, where you can access characters from the entire franchise. John says "It's a real time suck," and because it's approved for ages 12+, it's even safe for John.

The Un-App: Facebook

John got a great tip from John Federico, CEO of EventHero: "The browser version of Facebook is so good now I've deleted the Facebook app off my phone. I go a 25% battery boost because it's a massive battery drain. The Facebook app's energy usage is like leaving the A/C on in your house at 55° when it's 90° outside."

Prisma Photo Editor

What it does: Users can edit photos

Cost: Free, in-app purchases

https://apple.co/2MctQSM

This free app applies the style of different artists and effects to photos. The app won't turn less-than-great photography into great photography, but it can produce interesting results. There are hooks in the app for purchases, but you don't need to purchase anything to use the app.

John's black lab, Annie, agreed to model, so we could demonstrate the power of a couple of Prisma filters. Cool, right?

Tiny Piano Touchbar

What it does: User can "play the piano" on a MacBook

Cost: Free

This app isn't new, but Apple fans will enjoy entertaining their cube mates with a tune.

See it in action here: http://bit.ly/2w8wWfE

The app is free, but since it's not in the Apple App Store, it's "download at your own risk." http://www.utsire.com/touch-bar-piano/

All-Around Useful

NOAA Weather (National Oceanic and Atmospheric Administration)

What it does: Weather reporting

Cost: Free

http://mobile.weather.gov

The NOAA is the federal agency responsible for climate monitoring and other functions. John likes NOAA Weather for accurate weather reporting. You copy the URL to an icon on your phone's home page, and it behaves like an app, but no install is required; it behaves like an app on both iOS and Android. There are other weather apps that look better, but NOAA wins at accuracy.

Dark Sky

What it does: Hyperlocal reporting of precipitation

Cost: $3.99

https://darksky.net/app

This app made it onto John's phone, in addition to the NOAA weather app, because it predicts imminent rainfall or snow in more detail than most apps. It will say "It's going to start pouring in 15 minutes and stop raining in 35 minutes." It also shows you the % chance of precipitation on an hourly basis, which is hugely valuable. You don't realize that when

TV news says "60% chance of showers today" that could mean a 20% chance of showers all day (probably not going to rain at all), or a 100% chance of showers for you from 2-3pm (rain, but the entire day isn't lost).

Apple FaceTime Audio

What it does: Users are able to make calls

Cost: Free (only available and comes with Apple products)

Instead of making a cell call, John uses the FaceTime audio app. The audio quality is much better. Give it a try. Here are all the specs from Apple: https://support.apple.com/en-us/ht204380

Valt

What it does: Password management

https://valt.io/

Cost: Free, also Premium Version ($23.99/year)

John jumped to this app after interviewing Brent Heeringa, CEO and Co-Founder of Valt.

He said "I'm loving that it's so much easier to manage passwords than any other having to memorize a string of 16 characters."

To learn more about next generation multi-factor authentication, listen to this MoC podcast: http://bit.ly/2Mbyq3P

Nexxle

What it does: To-Do List

https://nexxle.com/

Cost: Free

John likes Nexxle because it's a great productivity tool with a lot of basic "to-do" functionality (like grocery lists). John likes how Nexxle allows you to share tasks, keep your projects in one space, and push the right tasks to the right people. It still has a few rough edges, the iOS version isn't out yet, and it doesn't integrate with platforms Google Calendar, or Trello. But Nexxle has replaced all of John's previous To-Do list apps.

Google Assistant

What it does: Hands-free communications

Cost: Free

http://bit.ly/2nARN7y

Google Assistant lives on Chris's phone home screen because of all the things it can do, including placing calls, generating texts, setting reminders in Google Calendar, etc. A huge side benefit is that it can send broadcasts to all the Google devices in his home; Chris uses that feature to broadcast his location ("Hey everyone, I'm in the basement!") Available for both iOS and Android.

MoviePro

What it does: Video recording and filmmaking

Cost: $5.99

https://apple.co/2nAC4FG

Chris likes MoviePro because the app lets him specify which mic to use when he's cutting video. According to Chris, if you don't specify which microphone to use, the native camera app tends to default to the built-in mic, which doesn't produce the best sound quality. For videos, Chris uses a headset with a Bluetooth connector that goes into the lightning connector, etc. for the best audio. MoviePro's color correction is good also for exposure control and white balance control, great for stepping up the look of your video.

Mindnode

What it does: Visual Goal Management

Cost: Free trial available, full-app $39.99 (with discounts if you own older versions)

https://mindnode.com/mindnode/mac

Mindnode is Chris's preferred tool for visual goal management. Below is one of Chris's maps for a Trust Insights client.

John: "I use my visual goal management tool for EVERYTHING: every project, personal goals, anything related to brainstorming or when I have a lot of unrelated content that I'm trying to unify."

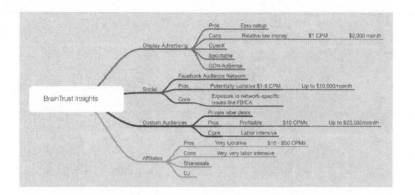

Chapter 7: Gear We Like aka Nerds R Us

Headphones/Headsets
Makes Life Easier
Personal & Home Tech
Gearhead Picks

John and Chris have fine-tuned their gear fetish almost into a spectator sport. But their compulsion is your gain, because we know they've subjected their gear purchases and reccos to the most onerous of circumstances: travel and children.

Headphones/Headsets
Johnny Headphones

The best headphones for webinars, video conferencing, or even just enjoying music.

http://JohnnyHeadphones.com/

John builds Johnny Headphones by modding the Sony MDR-7506 headphones. They are super comfortable and collapse neatly for transport.

Warning: You'll never go back to earbuds or other headphones, and your family may forget what you looked like without them.

Chris also likes Johnny Headphones: "I've found that this headset plus the microphone is fantastic for podcasting and doing audio recording on the go, they're also superb for webinars and conference calls. Also, I'll use just the microphone while I'm driving home from work to record memos and notes. Super useful when I'm on the road too."

KIMAFUN Wireless Headset for Video/Audio Recording

https://amzn.to/2I1B9KU

It's a headset, but Chris uses it for recording video stuff because it's one of the few that go straight into the iPhone, which produces superior audio. It can also plug into anything with a 3.5mm jack.

Chris said, "When I'm doing a content creation on the road, like speaking engagements, I'll wear this on-stage, wired directly into my phone. It produces top-quality audio from the stage, without any echoes. I'll excerpt footage from my session for YouTube and other media. And

because it's wireless, I'm not stumbling over 2 sets of wires on stage. The only downside is looking like an idiot on stage, because you're wearing both the event lavaliere microphone, and also the headset."

These headsets run about $50 for a 2.4 GHz paired adapter that plugs into your smartphone, you wear the other end. It also has a little belt pack body clip.

High-End Headsets

- Audeze LCD-3 ($1,945) https://amzn.to/2B8uWtR

- Sennheiser HD 800 ($1,599) https://amzn.to/2MkGUF0

- Sony MDR-Z7 ($699) https://amzn.to/2KSiFJA

John tested these 3 expensive headset for 3 weeks, rented from a now-defunct electronics website. If you're an entry-level audiophile, you might want to spring for the top 2: the Audeze and the Sennheisers. See John's detailed review on his blog: http://bit.ly/2MGyG6Z

If you're like John, you like good sound and comfort. But if you have other ways to spend $2K, stick to a workhorse like the Sony 7506 (better yet, get one of John's modded JohnnyHeadphones.)

V-Moda Headphones

https://amzn.to/2vIfuQ5

John says simply, "The V-Moda still rules."

If you have headphones that you already like, tack on recording capabilities for just $30 by adding a V-Moda plug-in microphone. For the price point, it just can't be beat, and it sounds amazing. John has tested over a dozen inline mics against the V-Moda, and even $150-200 mics don't measure up. They come with a 1-year warranty.

Makes Life Easier
TP-Link AV1000 1-Port Gigabit Powerline Adapter

https://amzn.to/2jFMHVJ

Chris: "I upgraded to the gigabit version. It's absolutely amazing stuff, and great for doing webinars from anywhere in the house. I've slapped up 4 of these throughout my home. There's one plugged by the nearest outlet to my router, and the others are plugged in throughout the house. The bandwidth is good, maybe not quite as good as running your own wire, but better than ripping open walls."

InDash Custom Dash Vehicle Mounts

http://bit.ly/2B8kUcb

John: "Got this from a favorite hard-core engineering site. Ripping up the dashboard for the wire mount was an interesting project. But I got sick and tired of suction cups mounted to the window, watching them fall in the winter and melt off in the summer."

Anker PowerCore 26800 Portable Charger

https://amzn.to/2rTKdab

Shift Communications gave away a gigantic 24,000 mAH power bank for the holidays a few years back (not this particular model) The power bank has a game-changing AC plug in the side, so you can plug-in your laptop if you're flying cross country or you're in a meeting or event, and here's no outlet nearby. At 24,000 mAH, it's the equivalent of 1-2 ½ refreshes of a standard laptop.

Personal & Home Tech
Google On-Hub Router

https://amzn.to/2nBFok1

Chris: "This router is super powerful. It may not be as fast as other routers, but its range is much better than most other routers. There are 5 rotating antennas inside the case which makes the router automatically directional. That means that once you tie your device (phone, laptop, etc.) to the router, the signal will follow you, no matter where you bring your device. I get a strong signal even through a couple of walls. Also, I can be in the anywhere in the backyard or outside the house and still have a good connection. It plays well with other Google devices, so all of my Google Home devices are connected to it. You can prioritize a certain device, for example, if your kids are rabid for bandwidth to power Netflix. Because Google created this router, I'm fully aware that Google is probably transmitting usage data back to the mothership."

Bose Pulse Wireless Headphones

https://amzn.to/2KN36nM

John: "I'm generally not a fan of wireless headphones, because Bluetooth is not as good as a cable, and batteries/recharging is a pain. But I love the Bose Pulse for working out because it has an integrated heart rate monitor on the left ear, so I've been able to give up the chest strap when I'm running. I use a FitBit surge on my wrist and found that a wrist based heart rate monitor isn't as good as the chest straps."

Fitbit Blaze

John is a fan of this fitness watch.

http://amzn.to/2AvlRcm

Bose SoundLink Revolve Portable Bluetooth 360 Speaker

https://amzn.to/2KMIxI2

John: "Technically, these portable speakers are on my wishlist. My birthday is in June, if anyone is so inclined."

B&H Photo & Electronics Corp.

http://bit.ly/BHPhoto-MoC

John: "I like to feed my tech addiction at B&H. Good selection of photo gear."

Amazon Alexa - Echo Spots

https://amzn.to/2ru6ECt

Chris: "My devices are plugged into my Amazon Prime music library. Also, I bought the Echo Spots because they have a little 2" video screen; they're great for quick, room-to-room video conferencing. You don't even need to run them out to an external speaker; they work well on their own."

John: "We've got Alexa down the kitchen. My wife and kids fight with her constantly. Alexa ignores my wife when she gets the syntax wrong, and my son calls her EE-lexa. And we all get a little frustrated at her inability to filter Christmas music in non-December months. But we're hanging in there…"

Microsoft Natural Ergonomic Keyboard 4000 for Business

Although you usually want to test-drive an external keyboard to ensure that it's a "fit," this keyboard is closest to the one that John uses for the desktop:

https://amzn.to/2vGUuci

MacBook Pro Laptop

Chris: "I have the MacBook Pro, upgraded to the one that has the touch bar. I love the touch bar and the touch ID to unlock stuff and authenticate. I'm not a fan of what they did with the ports. They're all USB-C ports, so now my dongles have dongles."

Google Home

http://bit.ly/2KPCn8J

John: "We've got a lot of Alexa usage under our belt, but if you've bought into the Google ecosystem, sprinkle a few of these around your home."

Travel Bag: Travelpro Platinum Magna 2 21" Exp Spinner Suiter

Overall, Chris likes this bag a lot. The wheels aren't perfect, but he likes the balance of the bag.

http://amzn.to/2jTcQA2

More details on Chris's blog: http://bit.ly/2B8Ay7i

Anker Roav Dashcam

https://amzn.to/2rol5c3

Micro SD card (you'll need one for the Dashcam)

https://amzn.to/2wkRg12

John: "Anker products are solid; Anker has a ton of fans because of their product quality."

Chris uses the Roav, and it does 4K recording on a micro SD card. He finds it super helpful for a couple of things:

1. If you're driving responsibly, with your hands around the wheel, that means you're not monkeying around with your smartphone. You may see an interesting sight, and think, "I should've taken a picture of that." You can log into the cam's mobile app and find that photo as part of the video taken during the journey. Keep in mind that the cam only runs when electrical power is being generated by the motor, i.e. not in park mode.

2. Your auto insurance company may be able to use the footage to prove accident causality, which may expedite your insurance claim. (NOTE: As of the book publication date, could not find any evidence of insurance discounts in the US.)

Nest Thermostat

https://nest.com/thermostats/nest-thermostat-e/overview/

John: "Not only does it look great, but I can use the app to check on the house temp remotely. It also knows when my phone leaves the house, and can turn down the temp (geofencing). And it stores history so I can see how long the furnace was running every day."

Gearhead Picks
Oculus Go

https://amzn.to/2rv3ApI

Chris: "It's supposed to be the cheaper version of the Oculus Rift headset, but it's still $200 for a single use device that your smartphone can do 80 percent as well for $0 extra dollars."

John: "One of these days, it's going to take off."

Pilot Erasable Ink Pens

https://amzn.to/2vOcqC3

The ink is heat-sensitive; the erase is made of hard rubber, and the heat of the friction against paper heats the ink and makes it disappear (NOTE: do NOT use for writing checks).

RocketBook

https://amzn.to/2P4hrOF

You can fill up the notebook; pop it in the microwave for 3 minutes to erase it entirely.

Raspberry Pi

https://amzn.to/2jTYnEv

John thinks that the Pi is great for messing around. The new one has Bluetooth and Wifi included. John likes to wax nostalgic about what life was like when keyboards, power and monitor cords were standard issue at home. If you want to flashback to when people owned "real" computers, you'll enjoy the Raspberry Pi (and please appreciate our restraint in not making a joke about having raspberry pi with your Marketing Over Coffee.)

Chapter 8: Stuff We Like (And We're Not Paid to Promote)

Cool Random Stuff
    Doing Well By Doing Good
    Star Trek White Noise Generator
    Insider Shopping Tip
    Little Known Purple One Recordings
    A Great Amazon Troll
    Now With More Voting!
Media and Ads We Like
    Watch-Worthy Ads
    Not Fake Media
Tech
    How to: Python
    Plugins We Like
    Schneier On Security
    Internet of Things Hacking Attack
    The Gartner Hype Cycle
    Amazon Drone Delivery
Travel Hacks
    Airline Hacks
    Where to Stay
    Where to Meet
Books We Like

Check out our cool marketing junk drawer!

Here's our unwittingly-curated collection of fun and random finds, along with more serious books, articles, and blogs. Get the benefit of our 256+ years of combined experience (yes, we're stealing that combined age cliché, even though it's probably closer to 40.) Seriously, when we run across something that is useful and time-saving, we like to spill the coffee beans on MoC.

Cool Random Stuff

Doing Well By Doing Good

It's not just about employee retention or employee productivity. Lori Magno, VP of Corporate Culture at Digitas (www.Digitas.com), the largest ad agency in Boston, MA, shared with us how Digitas creates opportunities for employees to bond with each other and the company.

Lori finds that enthusiasm for corporate culture initiatives spills into relationships with clients:

"We certainly share what we are doing with clients ...and we see them getting involved in various projects. The greatest thing ever is when our clients take note and say 'hey, this looks really interesting, how can we be a part of it?' We have clients who are interested in stepping up and expanding their missions. It's huge."

144

Star Trek White Noise Generator

Ambient Noise Generator, Star Trek edition, which makes the various background noises of the different starships, Enterprise and Voyager. It's free from MyNoise, a site that offers a ton of custom background noises: https://mynoise.net/noiseMachines.php

Insider Shopping Tip

John: "There are always fresher bananas by the checkout section than in the produce section, the ones by the impulse items don't get as picked clean as the produce section."

Little Known Purple One Recordings

John: "If you're a hardcore Prince fan, he did some jazz with a band called Madhouse, which doesn't have his name on their recordings. I was able to get it on a CD via a Japanese release sold on Amazon for just $45, even though I'd seen it sell from $100 to $500."

Here's one recording on YouTube: http://bit.ly/2Owdu4o

John said, "I probably should just resell it because I do not keep anything of value in my home. My kids will just destroy it, I'll find it underneath the rug for years or scratched beyond recognition. I need an underground bunker, some bombproof shelter."

Chris's advice: "Just put the CD in the helium-filled, underground vault to keep it safe, and hand it down to your kids."

Update: John did sell it, at a handsome profit of $55, thus doubling his money and foiling his kids from any inadvertent or intended destruction.

A Great Amazon Troll

Do not pass Go, do not collect $200, until you watch this entire 3:37 video from Amazon Web Services (AWS).

https://amzn.to/2P7D9Bx

Now With More Voting!

You can now register to vote online in many states. Register well in advance so you can vote from your computer. You can vote online instead of submitting absentee ballots. Search for "Online Voting" with the name of your state, and you'll be taken to the link if it's available in your state.

Media and Ads We Like

Watch-Worthy Ads

John is a fan of the Taylor Swift treadmill ad. It's got over 20MM views, and it exploded music sales for Drake. Taylor's a good sport, not afraid to play the fool (on April Fools' Day, when the ad premiered), while getting business done.

https://www.youtube.com/watch?v=fK_zwl-lnmc

Chris loves how the Cookie Monster ad is G-rated, completely safe for everyone. Both the original ad and the outtakes version are hilarious; it's totally worth the time to watch them. John says (just a bit cynically): "It's amazing how the linking back to childhood suddenly creates a whole emotional connection that can easily be played."

Cookie Monster "Hey Siri" ad:

https://www.youtube.com/watch?v=MF6OYq_2Ooc

Outtakes of Cookie Monster "Hey Siri" ad:

https://www.youtube.com/watch?v=_Wsp23UcqrU

John: "Lyft has done a bunch of ads with undercover drivers. I don't think that Shaq wearing a fake beard would fool anyone, but you'll get a chuckle out this ad":

https://www.youtube.com/watch?v=SJwrUaQvtsc

John: "If you're one of the 4 people on the planet that missed the Chewbacca Mask Lady meme, you owe it to yourself to watch. It's the most viewed video on Facebook, getting about 100MM of viewers within 1 ½ weeks."

https://www.youtube.com/watch?v=y3yRv5Jg5TI

Not Fake Media
British Broadcasting Corporation

http://www.bbc.com/news

The BBC is John's go-to source for trustworthy news. They're the bastion (maybe the last one) of old school journalism, with news based on fact. On Twitter: @BBCBreaking and @BBCWorld

NPR podcast: "Here's the Thing" with Alec Baldwin

Alec's podcast is impeccably produced in the NPR style, and covers politics, Hollywood, Broadway, and whatever else catches his eye. John has discovered some interesting episodes in the archived podcasts, including episodes featuring Jimmy Fallon, Carol Burnett, Amy Schumer, Bernie Sanders, Dustin Hoffman, Edie Falco, John McEnroe and more.

L2 Inc.

YouTube https://www.youtube.com/user/l2thinktank

Catch Scott Galaway on YouTube for his 4-minute wrap-ups on ecommerce, including his insight on retail and the state of the internet. He's just like us – educational and entertaining.

Tech

How to: Python

Python is an excellent platform for helping to organize and analyze a massive amount of data. Lynda (acquired by LinkedIn in 2015), an online education resource, is a great place to start: http://www.lynda.com/Python-training-tutorials/415-0.html

Plugins We Like

Chris and John want to give a shoutout to Yoast SEO's Glue plugin. The Glue plug-in ties into Facebook Instant Articles and Google AMP plugins to make sure that you're not at risk for duplicate content penalties. If you use Yoast SEO, they recommend you install it ASAP.

https://wordpress.org/plugins/glue-for-yoast-seo-amp/

Schneier On Security

https://www.schneier.com/

Bruce Schneier, a bona fide security technologist and author, writes a fantastic blog on security developments that could have significant real world implications. One of the blog posts reveals how wifi signals can be used to identify people by body shape. Bruce always has an interesting, cutting-edge take on things, so we recommend him highly.

Internet of Things Hacking Attack

The Internet of Things is quite possibly the largest hack bot network on the planet. Krebs on Security wrote a post about it and got taken down by a massive denial of service attack with datablasts of up to 620GB/second, which is unlike any other attack in hacking history.

Akamai, their DDoS protection provider, and Alchemy, their content provider or content caching network, dropped them because they couldn't handle the magnitude of the attack. Most of it came from 'smart' appliances, like refrigerators and toasters. When you have that much machine-to-machine communication with that many embedded devices that are that poorly secured, you're going to have a real serious hacking problem and no one is safe from it."

More details here: https://krebsonsecurity.com/tag/internet-of-things/

The Gartner Hype Cycle

"This report is always great. Gartner puts out this chart once a year, and it's a cool, visual shorthand for what's going on with emerging tech. The premise behind the chart is that some technologies get really hyped up in the press, and after that initial spurt, their press falls off. After a while, everyone starts to beat up these hyped technologies, because they're not an instant cure for cancer, won't make your dinner, etc. A lot of tech products end up in the "trough of disillusionment." But if there's really meat to the technology, eventually the tech succeeds in the marketplace (or gets bought), regardless of what the press says.

Marketers can use this chart to learn about new technologies in a few ways:

- Check out emerging tech prior to when management will ask about the technology at the peak

- Management asks you to look at tech which is at the pinnacle of the hype cycle, but hasn't been proven, i.e. made its way out of the trough

- Watch tech that's made it out of the chasm; if you're not using it, there may be some solid stuff there.

Take a look now: https://gtnr.it/2KPm5wM

Amazon Drone Delivery

Truly mind-blowing footage of an Amazon Prime delivery by drone: no human pilot, takes only 13 minutes from the time of online order to delivery. Worth watching: https://youtu.be/vNySOrI2Ny8

Travel Hacks

Airline Hacks

If you're a regular business traveler, definitely enroll in TSA Pre-Check or Global Entry for business travel. If you hit the airport at peak time, the non-Pre-Check line can be as long as 2 hours. Another tip: some credit cards will refund the TSA fee to your automatically. Good article at Business.com: http://bit.ly/2P7Fexl

Also, have you ever had to pay for airfare - and then immediately have to cancel your trip? Most airlines will process your refund without any fees if you ask for it no later than 24 hours from making the reservation.

Where to Stay

Start with AirBnB, not large hotels. Once hotels are filled up, people start to hit up AirBnB and homeowners jack up their prices. Get your reservation done before the price increase. That strategy doesn't always work, but it's worth a try. An AirBnB multi-room house is especially great for a small start-up team.

Where to Meet

www.Breather.com

John and Chris use Breather all the time. If you're in a major city and you need some office space, to have client meetings, or just to sit in a private space with a table, chargers (and access to a bathroom), Breather is a fantastic way to rent space by the hour. Julien Smith, their CEO, goes all the way back with John and Chris to PodCamp One.

Books We Like

"Disrupted: My Misadventure in the Start-Up Bubble" by Dan Lyons

https://amzn.to/2vGFdrN

For John's full review, visit his blog, Ronin Marketeer:
https://www.roninmarketeer.com/2016/05/03/regarding-disrupted/

John was fortunate to be able to talk to a lot of the players around the time of Dan's departure from HubSpot. As John admits: "Of course, a lot of my perspective is due to my own start-up PTSD, which I needed to get over." Although John expected some of the rumor mill to surface in the book, there are some legit topics covered in the book, such as startup culture, the treatment of workers over 40, VC and the state of our economy, and the unequal distribution of wealth implicit in startups. Because it's based on one person's experiences and expectations, it needs to be taken with a grain of salt. But it's a good read.

"Generation Creation: Creativity in the Age of Everything"

Bill Green, Angela Natividad, Darryl Ohrt

https://amzn.to/2NS8arQ

Bill, Angela and Darryl shared their incredible wealth of experience, and giving MoC listeners insight into ad agencies, and what it takes to hire and manage creatives.

Some of our favorites nuggets of wisdom:

Unusual = Fun = An Asset

Daryl, who started in the music business and morphed into the ad agency business, found that it's best to let people be comfortable and let them dress however they want to dress. Not only does fashion freedom help creatives produce their best work, it gives an ad agency an advantage. "Clients like to work with their agency -- it's their 'fun hour', because creatives don't dress and act exactly like bookkeepers and others typical business types," points out Angela. Bottomline: "Allow people to be themselves" to get their best work.

But When to Draw the Line

Angela observed that different countries, especially in Europe, have different standards for body hygiene (we're trying to be diplomatic here, but it boils down to cleaning frequency, with soap.) According to Angela, younger creatives need to sometime be educated on minimal acceptable grooming habits.

Chemistry v. Culture

The authors agree that there is only so much that culture can accomplish. Strong relationships precede culture, and bonds between the team players helps to overcome phenomenon like negativity and self-serving behavior. Ideally, chemistry leads to an organically-created culture that's mission-based. Don't depend on physical ways to create culture, like weekly group lunches or workout sessions.

Overall, great chemistry ⇒ great culture ⇒ the confidence and talent to create and sell great creative

Why Diversity is Easier Said than Done

Almost by definition, diversity in any form will make team members uncomfortable. It takes great, gifted leadership, to have the foresight to bring in diverse members that will add healthy debate and different world views to the team, while helping the team to nurture bonds of trust for the times when team members disagree. It helps to create a bigger, inspiring mission, and to teach employees how to trust each other's talents.

What Makes a Great Creative Director? A Checklist:

- Can recognize great creative

- Can build and foster a team that creates great creative (in other words, great creative doesn't usually doesn't come from one person)

- Can protect and sell great creative directive (perhaps the hardest part of the job)

- Can motivate and inspire people (will the team walk through fire for the creative director?)

- Is selfless, wants the rest of the team to succeed. Promotes everyone on the team

- Can edit --- In design, knows what to remove

- Is the "show runner" (knows how to make an idea take off, sees where the train is headed)

Agencies: Does size matter?

There is no magic number. Great creative can come from teams of 3 to teams of 100.

From the client side, you want to determine your exact needs. Bigger is not always better. Also, how quickly an agency is growing or hiring is not necessarily criteria for success.

Agency Red Flags

1. Beware of "vanity metrics," such as "We just worked the whole weekend!"

2. Make sure there is a very good reason for either very quick growth or very quick shrinkage.

3. Leadership needs to be adept at managing those significant types of transitions. In particular, hierarchical changes can be difficult to manage.

Mission: Live It or Die

More money and more staff will not fix a broken or insufficient agency mission. You need to see evidence of the agency mission, both from the client and employee sides.

"Value Based Fees: How to Charge - And Get - What You're Worth" by Allan Weiss

Chris calls this a "phenomenal book." The author shows how traditional hours/time/materials billing is not only a grind, but also unethical; it pits the interests of a consultant against their client. A better strategy: consultant and client agree to the value of the work upfront. Consultants and aspiring consultants: Read it. https://amzn.to/2P7GOiL

"Trust Me, I'm Lying: Confessions of a Media Manipulator" by Ryan Holiday

https://amzn.to/2B8XXWb

Chris gives extra points to the book's title; it's a media manipulation in itself. The book's core lesson is that publishing and journalism is entirely about page views now. And that means opening the wallet to throw ad dollars against syndicating media pieces, i.e. buying ads that promote content about your company on a publisher's web sites.

John agrees that the book "is fantastic." In a past MoC episode Ryan revealed a lot of the great stunts he pulled to drive up page views. (Still a great episode: find the 1/20/13 episode in the MoC archives, or listen here: http://bit.ly/2KP7LV5

Chapter 9: Now with More Interviews!

The Visionaries
> **Seth Godin**
> **Simon Sinek**
> **Christopher S. Penn**
> **David Meerman Scott**
> **Nick Westergaard**

Marketing Luminaries
> **Kipp Bodnar, HubSpot**
> **Scott Brinker, ChiefMarTech.com**
> **Allison MacLeod, Rapid7**
> **Seiya Vogt, Boxed (formerly of Bitly)**
> **Justin Mares, FOMO.com, also Kettle & Fire**

Social Media, PR and Alternative Media Experts
> **Jeremy Goldman**
> **Tim Street**
> **Tom Webster**

Customer Perception Virtuosos
> **Jay Baer**
> **Kate Edwards**
> **Daniel Lemin**

John began Marketing Over Coffee with a single goal: "I'll consider Marketing Over Coffee a success if I get to interview Seth Godin."

It took creativity and persistence, but John finally landed Seth as a guest in 2010. And even now, Marketing Over Coffee's most frequently listened-to podcast is an interview with Seth

Godin (and you, lucky reader, can read that interview in this chapter!)

With more than 10 years of interviews, John has had the great fortune to speak with an incredible roster of MoC guests. He's hosted everyone from forward-thinking visionaries and authors, successful entrepreneurs, industry observers, and fellow marketing execs.

But these interviews are more than entertainment. There's a ton of useful advice buried in these interviews, from the overarching, "What Are You Doing and Why," to the boots-on-the-ground, get-it-done stuff that you need to schedule. (If entertainment is more your vibe, Seth talks about his stereo set up.)

Our one piece of advice: scour these interviews for what applies uniquely to you and your organization.

For example, compare the B2B Marketing Case Studies from Allison MacLeod and Seiya Vogt. While Rapid7 and Bitly share basic B2B Marketing strategy and tactics, pay close attention to how each marketer understands their company's unique DNA, and how that DNA is best leveraged in marketing lead gen and conversion.

From John: "Thanks to everyone for all the great discussions. And keep the Star Wars, Star Trek, and gear recommendations coming."

The Visionaries

Seth Godin

Reinventing Professional Education

Looking back over my recent past, I've been seeking to reinvent education. I realize that's audacious, but I'm frustrated by two things:

1. Top-down, bureaucratic, accredited, credit-based diploma oriented education. It's overpriced and takes too long. It doesn't work very well, because you don't have emotional enrollment from the students in terms of them wanting to learn.

2. Expensive online courses that includes a bunch of videos. Many of the people who sign up are fooling themselves. They're not even buying a placebo. They imagine that watching videos is a substitute for doing the hard work of education. I've built some Udemy courses, and I'm proud of them. But I'm under no illusion that they're as effective as they could be.

That's why we started the altMBA, which is the most effective thing I've ever done. As of mid-2018, we've run 21 sessions. There's very little content; it's all about what you do how we walk as humans and engage at work. It does include marketing decision-making, finance, etc. I'm not in it, and there's no video of me.

altMBA students have a 96% completion rate because there's a life coach there all the time. The course completion rate of close to 100% is important to me, because I know that learning is difficult. If it were easy, everyone would be educated. College works because of peer pressure. If you're sitting in organic chemistry, surrounded by people who get it, you're more likely to work a little harder. If you're taking a course on calligraphy on SkillShare, you're watching a video, not learning calligraphy.

The Marketing Seminar was the second thing we built. I tried to build something that the audience was telling me they wanted: a little less emotional overhead and a little less personal accountability. It consists of 50 videos, with a lot of them delivered by me. It also has a discussion board with 1K+ people actively engaged with each other, talking about each lesson as it drips. People go at their own pace. We're not teaching algorithmic SEO, hustle, or hype marketing. We're teaching human marketing: how to get to real needs, desires and culture. The seminar is 10% of the cost of the altMBA, and the completion rate is not as high as the altMBA completion rate.

One of my favorite lessons revolves around the first 4 minutes of the movie "The Godfather". We put that scene up; I dissect it and explain the relationship between Don Corleone and the undertaker Bonasera, who asks the Don for a favor on the Don's daughter's wedding day.

Once you see how Coppola used tension in that scene, and the relationship between the lowly Undertaker and the Don, you learn a lesson about status roles and about the tension of saying yes, and saying no. I think that's about 10,000 times more important than understanding which keywords you ought to put in your next tweet.

The most difficult part of the courses is watching the videos, because it's not passive viewing. The student is required to write about the video, and give fellow students advice based on the video. That's where the actual hard work of learning occurs.

Education designed by Seth:

The altMBA: https://altmba.com/

The Marketing Seminar: https://themarketingseminar.com/

Seth on "First, Ten" and Social Media

My blog post called "First, ten" (https://seths.blog/2009/04/first-ten/) features this argument: everyone knows 10 people who trust them enough to try something. If you can deliver value to those 10 people, they'll tell their friends, and it will begin to spread. Our problem as marketers is not obscurity, it's that when someone encounters our idea, they don't care. And because they don't care, they don't take action. So getting people to care is more important than getting people to notice.

The problem with social media is that it's an engine based on the economics of getting people to notice. That's how Facebook and Google make all their money. And that's why people participate, so that they can notice and be noticed. I think noticing is way overrated.

If you win the noticing game, it is entirely possible to earn quite a good living, but it's a super competitive game. And there's just a few winners per category.

We know that when people do a search, only the top 2 results will benefit out of the 4K+ that may appear. On Twitter, just a few people have 1MM+ followers; most people have about 100 followers. It's difficult to be something that people don't care about, but that they engage with merely because it's popular. Popular people end up on magazine covers, and in the Fortune 500, so we think that's what everyone does. But the shift in most businesses, non-profits, and the culture don't come from the top down. The shift is a horizontal phenomenon which results from smaller groups of people who care."

The Customer's In Charge: Fallout

John: "We were talking with Healey Cypher who's talking about changes in retail by providing so much more service at the front end, recognizing every individual customer that comes in and creating better experiences. And so a term that's been kicked around is 'demassification,' where businesses are trying to emulate small businesses.

Seth: "Don Pepper and Martha Rogers wrote the book "The 1:1 Future" about 20 years ago. As far as I know, that was the first time that 1:1 marketing is introduced. Their model correctly predicted the 1:1 model (like Amazon), and that by a business knowing who the customer is, that knowledge was going to leak into every moment of a customer's life.

But I think Peppers and Rogers underestimated how emotionally difficult it is for business people to get their arms around this concept. Ironically, one of their biggest clients was Sears; one of the oldest marketers of their kind, with the #1 tool brand and #2 appliance brand. Sears lacked the humility to say, "We're not in charge anymore. The customer is in charge. We're not able to be a mass merchant anymore." And that shift is difficult for many institutions, because they'd rather insist that they're right, and continue business as usual, rather than respond to consumers being in charge."

Better Odds for the Big Guys?

Seth: "It's fascinating when you think about the Silicon Valley ethos, which is that the technologists show up and proclaim agnosticism, claiming we just write the algorithm and build the tool. It's not our fault that there's fake news. It's not our fault that the algorithm is punishing good businesses. It's not our fault that people are buying junk with one click.

But over time, the technologist usually realizes that it IS their fault, and that agnosticism is insufficient. They also recognize that there are continually newcomers who show up and make the case that they have a good idea that's worth consideration.

When Howard Schultz showed up, he wasn't a big guy. He was a little guy, but he believed in a user experience - a taste experience for everyone. Everyone said it wasn't going to work. But back to the "First, ten" concept: first you get 10 people, who get you 100 people, who get you 1K people, which makes the rules change.

So we're seeing that play out in retail, large and small. There's a store in New York City called Story. Rachel Schectman runs it completely differently than any other store. Every item is replaced every 6-8 weeks, with a new sponsor every 6-8 weeks. So it's programmed like a magazine, not like a store. That strategy would be unheard of by John Wanamaker in his day; it's the opposite of what you'd do if you're going to build a business that makes money when you sleep, because it's too much work." (A postscript: Macy's purchased Story in 2018.)

It's the same thing with a musician who jettisons the formula that made her last record a hit. She starts over again, because marketing isn't as persistent as it used to be, you can't coast on yesterday's success.

The Problem With the Invisible Hand

The Milton Friedman philosophy of the 'invisible hand' really angers me, because he gave greedy, fearful people the perfect crutch. They're greedy because they can make more money, and fearful because they weren't going to be responsible. In other words, if you're doing what you have to do -- raping, pillaging and maximizing profit -- because you have no other choice, then no one can blame you. But we're not comfortable letting people off the hook in any other space of our lives, so I don't think it's appropriate to let people off the hook here. I think it's the opposite; real creators and artists seek to be responsible by claiming ownership and owning the impacts of their creation. I think we ought to be able to hold CEOs and shareholders to the same standard.

Seth on Linchpins and AI

"My favorite definition of AI is: Everything a computer can't do yet. As soon as the computer can do it, we'll say, 'Oh, that's nothing but it'll never be able to do XYZ.' And that is dangerous, because we're fooling ourselves. Computers will keep getting better at doing the jobs of people who talk, and people who type, for a living. We didn't blink when robots start to do welding, because we're not welders. But now AI can read an X-ray better than a radiologist. It's going to happen to each of us.

The question is: Are you, as a creator, going to be able to reinvent and do something a computer can't do? For example, algorithmic advertising ought to be the enemy of everyone on Madison Avenue. Once you put a computer in charge of racing down the price curve and up the yield curve, we won't need people to do that anymore.

Most of the people you and I know are going to discover within the next 5 years that the thing we used to do all day doesn't need to get done now, so what are you going to do instead that creates value? Because if you're not creating value, if you're not a linchpin, someone is going to find someone cheaper than you to do it."

Why Seth Loves Subscriptions

Seth: "Yes, I love subscriptions. They're a big part of permission marketing, which I wrote in 1998.

Subscriptions have fallen out of favor because advertisers demand mass, which is what drives advertising revenues for most magazines, newspapers and TV. The advertiser's proposition: we will pay for the incremental cost of reaching an additional person, if the cost is low. So the bigger media, the better. Subscriptions weren't important, because they tend to decrease an audience's size. I've been arguing for 20 years that the 'bigger is better' approach is silly, because someone can always do mass better than you. But no one can do micro better than you; people who care about getting something they expect when they want it. And that we're happy to pay for it.

Doing it that ways makes us a customer, rather than a product, the way all of us are on Facebook. All the things in Facebook that you don't like are there because you're the product, not the customer. Twitter is a better example. When Twitter was about to go public, they could have chosen instead to charge their best users $10/month, and all of their power users would have happily paid. With 20MM power users paying $10/month = $2.4 billion/year and would prove the value that subscribers found in Twitter. But if instead, you need to be bigger, that means you have to embrace mass, shortcuts and noise.

If can you find at least 1,000 true fans who will happily pay you $10/month, you're done. That's all you need.

Seth on Siri, SEO, and Accepting No Substitutes

My wife hates Siri. And anytime Siri comes on, my wife screams at her, and my wife is not a screamer.

I think it's inevitable we'll add audio and voice to our experience of the net. We've maxed out on the time we can spend staring at a screen. We want to spend the rest of our time engaged. The problem is that audio is low bandwidth and linear. So you can scan a screen and see 20 things in a blink of an eye. But you can't scan a sound and you can't use it as a thoughtful multivariate interface.

I've never used a voice assistant it in a way that made me happy. But I think it's going to get one magnitude of order better in well under 5 years. I think we're going have a tough time remembering what it was like before it.

John: "Tom Webster pointed out that when you strip this down, i.e. low bandwidth and live interface, suddenly branding and the relationship returns. Someone using a voice assistant has to do the work of digging into their brain to describe what they want, and the personal relationship with a brand comes front and center."

Seth: "Yes, that's one of the lessons in The Marketing Seminar. SEO is what happens when a low-involvement search occurs. So if I type "plumber, zip code 10706," I don't care which plumber, I just want a plumber near my house and I will cede the decision to somebody else. If you're a marketer that's a tough thing to stomach, because if you don't win that search, you lose completely.

The alternative to low-involvement SEO is to be asked for by name. For example, don't give me any cookie, give me an Oreo cookie. If someone does an online or audio search for an Oreo cookie, Oreo wins every time.

That's going to be the battle: How do we get people to care **enough** to ask for us by name? People don't care **enough** because we ran ads. They'll care **enough** because there'll be a pre-established attachment: cultural, tribal, social or experiential attachment that makes people accept no substitutes.

Godin's Stereo Gear

Seth: "I listened to my stereo last night with a huge grin on my face, because I don't know how to make it better. We have

168

DeVore 0/96 high efficiency speakers, made by hand in Brooklyn, hooked up with a funky, inexpensive cable to a Shindo amp, handmade in Japan by Ken Shindo. That's being powered by the PS Audio DAC, made in Boulder, CO by Paul McGowan. That's all hooked up to my Mac with Roon software, which is the best software value in my life. It does a better job with your music and discover, and I think it makes music sound great.

Devore: https://www.stereophile.com/content/devore-fidelity-orangutan-o96-loudspeaker

PsAudio: https://www.psaudio.com/

Roon: https://roonlabs.com/

Shindo: The good news is that Ken Shindo's son took over the business. So if you're looking for a $12,500 pre-amp (a box you put between your turntable and your amplifier), you can still buy them. You can't get them online; if you go through the Shindo labs site to the US importer you can make an appointment. http://www.shindo-laboratory.co.jp/Front/indexe.html

Story here: https://www.stereophile.com/content/listening-177-shindo-monbrison-preamplifier

@ThisIsSethsBlog

Simon Sinek
Start With Why

https://amzn.to/2ztktpv

Simon admits that "all my work is about my own struggles in my own journey and my own one to understand the world around me in my own experiences." Also, "my books challenge people's perspectives. They offer a new way of seeing the world or how business works or how we interact, and they're based on research in biology, anthropology, and other fields of research."

"Start with Why" was born out of my own struggle to rediscover my passion. In a rapidly changing world, everyone needs to be a leader, to think of the bigger game and to reinvent themselves.

Leaders Eat Last

https://amzn.to/2MmvvV9

"My book 'Leaders Eat Last' was born out of few experiences. As my career started to grow, I started to struggle with knowing who to trust. I also spent time with people in the military, and was blown away how much they care about and love each other. In business, we have colleagues and coworkers. In the military, they have brothers and sisters. It's a different relationship. I discovered that I didn't want colleagues and coworkers. I wanted brothers and sisters, so I set out to understand what causes trust and cooperation. How do you take an idealized cause, and build an amazing culture that brings people together, but enables you to function in the real world?"

Together Is Better

https://amzn.to/2nBd8Oh

"I wanted to do something that was a departure from my usual book. And I wanted to do something delightful. People may buy it for themselves, but it's designed to be given away. It's based on research, and the message is that we need each other. It's fully illustrated, and it can be read in about 15 minutes. My hope is that it will be a 'thank you' gift."

Find Your Why

https://amzn.to/2KS4AM7

We haven't reviewed this one yet!

How Game Theory Is Applied to Companies

Simon is fascinated by Game Theory, and two types of games: finite and infinite games. His new book, "The Infinite Game," is scheduled for the end of 2018, and we hope to speak with him about it soon:

https://amzn.to/2P6qkao

In a finite game, there are known players, fixed rules and agreed-upon objectives. For example, in baseball, we know who's on the roster, we know the rules, and we've agreed that whoever has more runs after nine innings is the winner.

An infinite game has both known and unknown participants. The rules are changeable and the objective is to perpetuate the game.

When you pit a finite player against a finite player, the system is stable. Using the above example, baseball is stable.

When you pit an infinite game player against an infinite player, the system is also stable, because there's no such thing as a winner or loser in an infinite game. Infinite games only end when players drop out because they've run out of the resources or the will to stay in the game.

In game theory, problems arise when you pit a finite player against an infinite player. Finite players are playing to win, and infinite players are playing to stay in the game.

Game theory also applies to finite v. infinite orientation of companies

Finite players are obsessed with their competition, and being #1 based on arbitrary standards, such as revenues, market share, and profit. Even looking at annual results are arbitrary.

Infinite players are focused on where they are going, how to be better and how to advance their cause. They understand that you don't win every game, and you can still be the champion at the end of the season. And you don't have to fight to win every battle. It's all about advancing the greater idea. And infinite companies are not confined by a 1-year game -- they can be looking at a 5-year game, 10-year game, a game without any defined end. Invariably, companies and leaders that play the infinite game frustrate their competition.

An example of an infinite player is Apple. At an Apple conference, 100% of the execs spend 100% of their time talking about how to help teachers teach and how to help students learn.

How Game Theory Applies to People

An easy way to look at it: Your first name is your finite game. Your last name is your infinite game.

You will live until you die. But your family name will live on. You want to uphold the values and sacrifices made by those who came before you. And you want that name to exist beyond you and have a positive meaning.

There's nothing wrong with advancing your life or your career. But what's the thing that you will be remembered for? What's the thing that your children will carry on after you? What's the thing that your employees, your coworkers, your friends, your clients will carry on without you?

I had the opportunity to sit down with Richard Branson. I asked "How should I judge you when you're gone? Is it what you built with Virgin, and that you are an amazing entrepreneur?" Branson replied: "Don't judge me by anything I've done at Virgin. If you want to judge anything that I've done in my life, judge me by the quality of my children." In other words, judge me by the quality of the thing that will live on beyond me.

Balancing Short-Term v. Long-Term

It's simple, but not easy.

Don't kid yourself that making expedient decisions to fulfill today's needs and wants will put you on the path to success. That terrible client who you hate, but they're willing to pay? You know they're not going to be a long-term, loyal client. Even when you need to pay the bills, there's a point at which you have to "take the hit," and sacrifice awful clients to find the clients that will be the best long-term. Eventually, that discipline translates into freedom: the freedom to work only with the clients that you love.

People told me: "Simon, you can afford to do that." My response: "I've been making decisions this way even when we had no money. We turned down business because there were the people we didn't want to work with. We made short-term sacrifices to make our long-term beds. Other people do the opposite. They make short term bets and it comes out of long-term costs."

It's definitely simple. And not easy.

@SimonSinek

Christopher S. Penn

Trust Insights

Leading Innovation

http://www.christopherspenn.com/leading-innovation-book/

(Buy it direct from Chris for only $9.99. On Amazon, it costs $77.00)

You gotta love John's testimonial: "Having worked with Chris for so long, I've heard all the great stories over the years. For folks who haven't worked on a project with you for 8 years, they can get all the stories and advice in one easy book and save a bunch of time."

It's no spoiler to reveal that the words "Boredom" and "Blindspots" figure prominently in the "Leading Innovation" Table of Contents. Chris melded together his work history, voracious reading, and personal interests to produce his observations on innovation:

* What is innovation?

* How does it work?

* Why do you need it?

* How you make it happen inside your organization?

Lesson #1: Tales from the Stone Age (circa 1990)

Chris: "I was a summer intern at the old AT&T, when it was a 100% landline company. I worked for the 'win-back' division, a 50-person division dedicated to finding out the number of people who came back to AT&T from MCI and Sprint.

Each day, they printed out a confidential, 700-page spreadsheet report with the win-back info. The first day, I spent 7 ½ hours leafing through the data, attaching post-it notes, etc.

At the end of the day, I said, 'This is stupid.'

I asked to get the spreadsheet by email. Excel has a scripting language: Visual Basic. It's not the world's best programming language, but the winback number was in the same cell on every page.

I wrote a script that pulled the info from all the pages and tabulated the data I needed. I turned an 8-hour job into a 15-minute spreadsheet project with a simple bit of programming, which would ultimately save hundreds of hours of manual labor. (And at the end of the summer internship, they asked me to train my replacement because I'd been doing such a great job.) It was a classic example of innovation."

The Plus (+) Path

According to Chris, what makes us innovative isn't solely our core skill set, the skill set you usually think of as being required in your profession.

It takes skills and knowledge from outside your profession to get on the "Plus Path" to innovation. Your skills and knowledge can come from almost anywhere: prior or unrelated jobs, hobbies, studying or life experience. The key to innovation is combine your non-work skills and knowledge with your core skills.

Let's use Chris as a case study. Chris is a technologist with an extraordinary level of marketing know-how and experience. And Chris also knows a lot about:

- Martial Arts

- World of Warcraft

- Buddhism

- Programming (Chris admits to being an average programmer)

Chris found some unexpected intersections between his skill sets and knowledge base. For example, Chris has combined strategy from the World of Warcraft with his business experience to come up with business strategy. One of his Plus Paths looks like this:

Business experience + World of Warcraft Knowledge = Business Strategy

To figure out your Plus Path to innovation, experiment with how you combine your core skill set and work experience with other areas of experience and knowledge.

What is the Right Environment for Innovation?

Chris's philosophy on figuring out the right time to innovate is inspired by one of his favorite books on strategy:

"Your Strategy Needs a Strategy" by the Boston Consulting Group (BCG)

https://amzn.to/2vJ9OFh

BCG learned that companies can be classified into one of 5 environments, each with an associated strategy:

Classical: I can predict it, but I can't change it
Strategy: Be Big

Adaptive: I can't predict it, and I can't change it
Strategy: Be Fast

Visionary: I can predict it, and I can change it
Strategy: Be First

Shaping: I can't predict it, but I can change it
Strategy: Be The Orchestrator

Renewal: My resources are severely constrained
Strategy: Be Viable

Using this framework, the key to the strategy and innovation is knowing which of the 5 environments applies to your company. Sometimes, innovation is the wrong choice. For example, in the renewal environment, you're struggling to keep the lights on, so your focus is on cash generation and management, as well as relentless and ruthless execution of the basics. That's the wrong environment for introducing innovation. Once the business is out of trouble, innovate new solutions.

The Difference between Innovation and Creation

The Latin root of the word innovation is" innovare" (to renew or restore). The core concept behind innovation is to take something old, and turn it into something new. In contrast, creation is making something from nothing. While innovation and creation are related, and the practices for measuring each are similar, they're not the same.

The iPod is a good example of a product innovation. MP3 players existed long before the iPod, but they were hard to use. Steve Jobs figured out the importance of design, and the innovative iPod grew to dominate the MP3 player market.

EventHero (http://EventHero.io) is an example of an innovative software solution. (John still works for EventHero, so yes, it's a shameless plug.) EventHero took the mundane task of badge-scanning, and innovated it into app form, so that exhibitors can scan badges, perform lead retrieval and multi-session tracking that integrates with Eventbrite.

The LEAD Innovation Framework

4 Steps to Innovation:

#1 Learn

#2 Experiment

#3 Adjust

#4 Distribute

This framework is contrary to the view that most organizations have of innovation. The organization identifies 1-2 people who have a habit of "going rogue" and who like making new stuff. The organization then labels those people as "innovators," and makes them responsible for innovation. Nice theory, but it's not sustainable or scaleable.

Chris's 4-step innovation framework provides a structured, repeatable approach to innovation. When companies fail to innovate, they generally fail during the first two steps.

Barriers to Step #1: Learn

It's difficult to create something new out of something old if you don't have something old. The example Chris gives in his book: your culinary creativity is limited if the ingredients in your house are mac and cheese mix, milk and butter. Without any other ingredients, you're having macaroni and cheese for dinner.

In business, your ingredients are your people: their skill sets, their knowledge, their experience. If you're not investing enough in people, and/or your people don't invest in themselves by reading, blogs, social media, books, listening to podcasts, going to training, your people will have very thin toolboxes. That dearth of input undermines innovation because you have nothing old from which to make something new.

Barriers to Step #2: Experimentation

And Chris doesn't mean the "throw it against the wall and see if it sticks" type of experimentation. He means testing new things using the scientific method:

1. Create a hypothesis

2. Test the hypothesis (A/B split or other statistically-accepted structure)

3. Refine hypothesis based on test results

4. Retest

Companies tend to get experimentation wrong for one of two reasons: either they don't use the scientific method, or there's so much risk aversion and/or punishment of failure, it makes innovation unsafe.

Innovation is inherently risky; it takes insight and guts. The innovator needs to go out on a limb and say: "I'm going to stick my neck out, take a calculated risk, and say we should test this."

One caveat: The higher up you are in your organization, the bigger the career risk if you engage in innovation. But the higher up you are in your organization, the bigger the risk you can assume, because you have more authority.

Barriers to Steps #3 Adjust

There tends to be fewer barriers to these steps. People are more comfortable with adjusting or fine-tuning an innovation, mostly because it's not as risky as coming up with the innovation in the first place.

Barriers to Step #4 Distribute

Technology has torn down a lot of barriers to communicating an innovation and scaling it to the rest of the organization. New innovations can be communicated via meetings, videos, iPad apps, intranets, emails, etc.

Here's Chris' deck on innovation:

https://www.slideshare.net/MarTechConf/scaling-innovation-by-christopher-penn

We may be a little biased, but we think "Leading Innovation" is a great book and a steal at $9.99. The advice Chris shares from his martial arts teacher is worth at least that much. It's not in libraries, so download it into your Kindle or reading device.

@CSPenn

David Meerman Scott

The New Rules of Marketing and PR: How to Use Social Media, Online Video, Mobile Applications, Blogs, News Releases, and Viral Marketing to Reach Buyers Directly

https://amzn.to/2vKmX0M

"Marketing can create a piece of content, such as a YouTube video, that can communicate with a prospect at just about at the point when the prospect is ready to engage with the salesperson, but the prospect isn't quite sure yet.

"I'm a fan of live streaming video, such as Periscope and Facebook Live, as sales and marketing tools which leverage content to drive thousands of people into your brand. They can help close the deal. A great example can be seen for the Fluidstance Level, one of the coolest things in my office. It helps my body remain active while doing computer work at my standing desk. I bought it based on the really cool video on Indiegogo. Within a few minutes, I coughed up more than $200 to a start-up company based on the video alone."

http://bit.ly/2w6jcSN

More good advice from David: "If public appearances are part of your Marketing and PR arsenal, mastering the art of the selfie is key. It allows you to control the selfie background, the selfie image, and sometimes, can speed up the selfie process.

It's best to have your 'celebrity' (President, CEO, Company Spokesperson, etc.) take control of the selfie situation by taking the phone from your fan (conference attendees, customers, visitors, etc.), and then snapping the photo, and giving the phone back to the person. With enough practice, your celebrity can stage these selfies in as little as 10-30 seconds each. If your celebrity is out in the public eye often, get them used to taking selfies with both iPhones and Android cameras. It's the best way to control the quality and orientation of the selfie -- and watch your photo spread on social media.

@DMScott

Nick Westergaard

Get Scrappy: Smarter Digital Marketing for Businesses Big and Small

https://www.amazon.com/dp/0814437311

Nick has been working on helping companies with their marketing, all the way from small companies to the Fortune 500. We find his viewpoint "you need get more effective with fewer resources" refreshing and practical.

The Myth of Big

If you work for a small company, it's easy to think that only big brands with big budgets and   teams can do big things. But in Nick's experience, all companies, big or small, struggle with insufficient marketing resources. Nick likes to quote Samantha Kraemer, Digital Marketing Manager for Schwinn Bicycles: "We could all do with a few more people or a few more dollars."

Nick cautions against "chasing the wrong thing," the idea that "going big," whether in terms of technology, hardware, screen, even physical space, will magically solve budget or marketing problems.

Instead, Nick commends "scrappy marketers" who achieve effectiveness by making the most of available resources -- for example, combining freeware and social media tools with paid solutions.

According to Nick, there are smart steps you can't skip:

The Business Objective Reigns Supreme

It's tempting to see "shiny new things" as solutions. But that's the tail wagging the dog. Define your goal first and then determine how to accomplish it.

An example is involvement in social networks. We all want those cool icons on our website. And your management and colleagues may be talking up the newest social media (it seems like overnight, "everyone is on it.")

But that's just a form of peer pressure on marketers. You have to figure out which social media satisfies your business objective, and not get seduced by "the shiny new thing."

That's why it's best to have a written, reported marketing strategy. It will help you to defer random marketing suggestions.

Connecting Your Digital Dots

Scrappy marketers can and must perform software integration. You're bombarded with marketing messages, so it's critical that your outreach is synchronized and your systems are talking to each other. When you integrate solutions more effectively, it allows you to "punch above your weight class."

Ageism and the Social Media Unicorn

Digital natives are immersed social platforms; they understand the platforms and have years of experience in using them. But we misattribute this immersion as a set of "magic beans" that can be sprinkled on a business. The drawback is that digital natives can often be missing the business context.

Research has shown that what makes digital natives successful at their jobs aren't necessarily deep technical skills. Interpersonal, relationship, and content development skills are more important to job success. And according to a report by Altimeter, the most important skill set is the ability to multi-task and to accomplish internal initiatives.

So if you have a "get the young person and they'll automatically know what to do" mentality, dump that worldview. Make sure that younger hires have the communication and content skills needed to be successful, and integrate them with their older, more experienced colleagues who know the business.

The Question Bank

Questions can be one of your most powerful strategies to spark better conversation and engagement, especially social media. Research shows that if you ask a question, it creates the need for an immediate, active response from the listener. Not only will your questions generate responses, you may uncover unmet needs.

Answers to effective questions can put you on the path to creating more interesting and useful content. Examples include:

What is your favorite example of _____?

What does _____ remind you of?

Don't depend entirely on Marketing to come up with good questions. Get your customer reps and field sales people to find out what customers are struggling with.

Store questions in a "Question Bank," so it's available to your entire company. You don't need a sophisticated solution. Evernote, Google Docs, BaseCamp and similar tools work well.

Brand Still Matters

Although the marketing "megaphone" has changed dramatically, what hasn't changed making sure you have a brand behind that megaphone: a brand that stands for something and has a unique story. Nick says: "As we have all these new tools, It is more important than ever to make sure that you know what your story is. Sometimes I think that we rush to the megaphone; it may or may not connect back to your mission. Everything works better when it is all connected."

For Trekkies

John relies on Nick's Facebook page to stay up-to-date on the latest Star Wars/Trek News:

https://www.facebook.com/nickolaswestergaard

@NickWestergaard

Marketing Luminaries

Kipp Bodnar, HubSpot
7 Key Marketing Insights

1. Make CRM Work for the Salesperson (Not Just Sales Management)

"We're focusing on bringing a full box CRM to the market, including pre-populated data, autolog calls, and other things to save a salesperson's time. Providing reporting and insight for sales management puts the onus on salespeople and requires a lot of effort. Cutting out some of that work give Sales Management the data they need, but makes the reps life easier, so they can be more productive, and hopefully, earn more money.

2. Make CRM work for the Prospect

"On the CRM front, our meetings applications enables the marketer to have an app right on their site. Instead of a prospect having to fill out a form, the prospect can book a meeting with a rep just using the app. It's great for the prospect, because frankly, we're removing friction from the process.

We also offer a 'Collected Forms Tool' as part of our free trial offer (see below). It allows the marketer to do great data capture and conversion, right on the web site. We've integrated LinkedIn into our free CRM product, so there's a smooth flow: anonymous web visitor -> lead ->contact in your CRM-> engagement.

3. Artificial Intelligence (AI) and the Democratization of Marketing

"I think it is probably, long-term, the single biggest impact to the marketing profession," said Kipp.

"With the fast pace of AI evolution and natural language processing, we're going to be able to do a lot of the tasks that you need a big marketing team to do. Natural language processing is kind of one of the big holdups. It's still really hard to get information in a way that a computer can parse it and interpret it quickly and easily. Companies that have larger sets of data, and more specific sets of data, have a real advantage in those areas because they can train NLP faster, they can build their machine learning algorithms faster."

4. AI and Social Media -- Who dominates, and how?

"If you're an objective observer of the marketplace, you'd say is that Facebook and Snapchat are innovating their platforms fastest. Especially on the bot side of things, Facebook Messenger is massive. Facebook for Work being available to the masses is going to have a big impact. I think Facebook is the dominant player in that market. They'll need to figure out the mechanics to enable users to interact, as well as how to discover bots.

Can Facebook and retailers play well together? I buy some of my clothes from a company called Everlane. The entire process takes place on Facebook: order suggestions, shipping confirmations, etc. Everything takes place via FB Messenger."

5. Account Based Marketing (ABM) -- When does it work best?

"Advertising is a big channel in ABM, it may seem counter-intuitive. I think it's an effective strategy if you have a very small customer base --- there's a total hundred companies in the world that are ever going to purchase your product. You've got to work on building great relationships with folks at those companies, as well as trust, loyalty, and brand recognition."

6. International Marketing Technology Adoption

"If you use the U.S. as a barometer. Latin America is probably 3 ½ years behind the states in their adoption of marketing technology and practices, especially when it comes to the web. Areas like Singapore and Southeast Asia are far ahead in use of messaging applications and a lot of other different communications channels, but they're still not using a lot of marketing technology. They're still figuring out how their strategy is evolving, and then technology decisions flow from that. In America, most marketers realize they need a stack of tools."

7. It's Time to Graduate from Excel

According to Kipp, a lot of great companies are still using Excel as their principal CRM tool. "We think that a CRM system is a better way to go, especially when it comes to collaboration, scale, and data --- and did we mention that the small business, lead-in version is free?" HubSpot CRM

https://www.hubspot.com/products/crm

8. Big Data and NLP

Kipp explained: "We're looking at which data can we collect through our customers' interactions, and their use of the our product to help us provide them with a better experience over time.

Companies with larger and more specific data sets have a real advantage in NLP and AI because they can train NLP and build machine-learning algorithms faster. HubSpot wants to provide a better customer experience. Amassing tons of data because we might need it down the road is not a practical use of our time. We want to be really focused on supporting and helping the customer base long term."

@KippBodnar

Scott Brinker, ChiefMarTech.com

Hacking Marketing: Agile Practices to Make Marketing Smarter, Faster, and More Innovative

https://amzn.to/2JjDxKr

Chief Marketing Technologist (MarTech) Blog

https://chiefmartec.com/blog/

Scott Brinker is one of John's go-to gurus when it comes to the intersection of marketing and technology. If you've ever wondered if marketing software vendors are breeding like rabbits, birthing an exponential number of new, baby martech solutions --- well, Scott explains the facts of martech life to MoC.

"My blog, Chief Marketing Technologist (MarTech) https://chiefmartec.com/blog/ was launched in 2008. I was inspired by the increasing invasion of marketing departments by people with technology backgrounds who love marketing."

The goal of "Hacking Marketing" is to provide a crash course in the ideas from the software world that you can adapt to marketing. Most marketers don't have a background in software engineering, and they don't necessarily need that background, but their livelihood now requires a basic understanding of how tech works. And more importantly, they need to rethink how to manage marketing, given all these software dynamics.

On today's career spectrum, software people would be at one end of that spectrum and marketing people would be at the opposite end. I speak with many organizations where people from the marketing and tech groups are intermingling. People are proud of having a little bit of both of those talents, and thinking about how to connect the dots between them.

I initiated my Marketing Technology Landscape Infographic in 2011, including about 150 tools. The purpose of the infographic was to show companies "Here's why you want technologists in the Marketing Department; your business is dependent on finding and leveraging the right tools effectively."

The original infographic, updated on an annual basis, has exploded into the 2018 MarTech 5000 Supergraphic, with 6,829 companies categorized into 6 categories: Advertising & Promotion, Content & Experience, Social & Relationships, Commerce & Sales, Data, and Management.

(If you have not yet seen the MarTech Supergraphic, you must remedy that right now: https://chiefmartec.com/2018/04/marketing-technology-landscape-supergraphic-2018/)

The MarTech Conference was launched in 2014; the show currently runs on an East Coast/West Coast schedule, with 100+ marketing technology exhibitors. More info here:

https://martechconf.com/

Why the Explosion in MarTech?

Says Scott: "The MarTech space is fascinating. You could ask 10 different people and get 10 different theories on why it is the way it is, and how it's going to move forward.

I see two primary forces that have driven the landscape:

1. **Expanded Marketing Scope:** Marketing is increasingly responsible for the customer experience. Compared to 10 years ago, Marketing is responsible for 10X more potential touchpoints. There are so many more opportunities for software solutions -- especially digital; they're ideal for software solutions.

2. **Ease and Economics of Software Development:** Thanks to the SaaS model, it's far easier to build and market software. Amazon, Microsoft, and Google offer so many tools and resources that help developers. Two people in a garage can conceptualize a marketing solution, build it, market it, and sell into early adopter brands. That process is not folklore; it does and can happen easily."

A great example of software that solves a very specific marketing problem easily is Vidmob (www.vidmob.com), a movie/video creation service. You upload your raw video footage and media into the cloud; their contractors edit the content into videos.

https://itunes.apple.com/cg/app/vidmob/id1054391136?mt=8

Software companies do not breed, but...

Scott: ""The MarTech 5000 Supergraphic we publish makes marketing technology companies appear equal; due to space constraints, all the company logos are tiny.

In reality, I see 3 levels of Martech companies:

Tier 1: Huge Enterprise Companies

Adobe, Oracle, Salesforce, etc. They're not going anywhere, and they're the major players in the MarTech space.

Tier 2: Venture Backed Companies

The companies in this space are very exciting, and have received significant venture funding. Companies in this tier can be acquired by a Tier 1 enterprise, or they stay independent, but their growth trajectories tend to be fixed when they're in this tier.

An example of a Tier 2 company was Infer, a frequent Marketing Over Coffee sponsor, before they were acquired by ESW Capital LLC, to operate as part of the ESW affiliate Ignite Technologies, Inc.

Tier 3: Everyone Else

The last layer of companies is in a free-for-all. Some of these companies will ascend to Tier 2 and/or be acquired by larger companies higher up in the ecosystem. But there's so much innovation, so quickly, that some of Tier 3 companies aren't able to find a sufficiently stable market, or any market, and they go out of business.

The Scrappy Niche-Players: It doesn't require very much money to run many software-based businesses, so the economics required for success are radically different from the past.

If a company is able to find a niche audience or works with a set of brands or agencies who love them, that makes the company a viable businesses. That type of small, niche-solution company may not appeal to VCs, (i.e. not the next billion dollar unicorn). But a small, profitable software company can succeed by not taking on any debt, while serving their clients and providing a vocation for the company's staff. Nobody's pushing them to go beyond what they do well."

John: "Here's an example of a scrappy niche-player and a shameless plug: https://eventhero.io you know what to do."

@ChiefMarTec

Allison MacLeod, Rapid7
B2B Marketing on Steroids: A Case Study

Over the years, we've conducted interviews with many of the "best of the best" in B2B marketing. This case study is based on two interviews with Allison MacLeod of Rapid7:

Marketing Over Coffee:

http://www.marketingovercoffee.com/2016/05/06/allison-macleod-from-rapid7/

Stack and Flow (MoC's sister podcast):

https://stackandflow.io/episodes/allison-macleod-rapid7/

We're providing this relatively detailed case study, because we think it encompasses many of the "best in breed" marketing philosophies and execution. *Warning: The case study is not short. For good reason. So if you've been subsisting on a steady diet of FB posts and Twitter tweets…..well, you've been warned.*

Rapid7, www.Rapid7.com, is a Boston-based IT security company. Rapid7 debuted on the NASDAQ in July 2015 (RPD). The company helps customers understand and utilize their security data to predict areas of IT security vulnerability, how to stop breaches as they're happening, and speed up investigations of IT breaches. Rapid7 also helps customers develop their security roadmap and security teams.

Overarching Principle: The Customer

As you read through this interview, keep in mind one dominant theme: Rapid7 maintains strategic and consistent focus on the customer: who are they and how to make them successful. This orientation pervades all aspect of their marketing: from organization to strategy to execution. Rapid7 also has a sophisticated view of the customer, recognizing multiple entry points and motivations.

Organization: Sales/Marketing and Domestic/Global

Sales & Marketing are separate, but they work extremely closely together. There is a CMO of Marketing, and an SVP of Sales.

Rapid7 has grown rapidly from about 200 employees in 2012, to about 800 employees in 2016 (increase of approximately 400%).

The marketing team grew as well: in 2012, there were 10 people on the Marketing team. Four years later, in 2016, the Marketing team grew to a global team of 45, spread between 5 different teams. (As of mid-2017, the Marketing team grew by 5 to 50 people).

Note: For those interested in benchmarking, the employee growth figures indicate that by 2016, Rapid7's marketing team grew slightly faster than the corporate team overall: marketing grew by 450%, compared to overall corporate growth of 400%

Originally, Allison had 3 people on the Marketing team. The responsibilities were organized as follows:

Employee 1: Demand

Says Allison: "In terms of our go-to-market and demand teams, we're aligned by solution area and area of the business of which we market and sell to."

Employee 2: Marketing Operations

Employee 3: Digital (SEO and Paid media)

"We think of the top of the funnel in terms of our search, our digital marketing -- that's more of a skill base across the entire business.... How do we grow website traffic? How do we capture potential buyers and customers? How to convert them?"

At the level of 15 marketers, Marketing is focused on the whole customer lifecycle, everything from inbound marketing and digital channels, to driving awareness at the top of the funnel, the demand team, and ultimately through to the Business Development Representatives (see BDRS below). The team is organized by both skill set (for example, digital skills, operational skills) and also by alignment to the sales organization.

Global Marketing: There is a global Marketing Director counterpart to Allison (who, at the time of publication is the director of the US marketing team). The global marketing team handles mix of everything handled in the U.S. but focuses on India and Asia Pacific. The US digital marketing team provides support globally, to all of the marketing organizations, such as SEO, inbound traffic and digital advertising. See Global Marketing below for more info.

Web Site

According to Allison, the Rapid7 web site is "a workhorse. As we're driving people through the top of the funnel, we're really looking at the quality and not the quantity piece. We want to be more in the business of how are we driving customers that want to engage with us, and potential buyers.

Rapid7 uses Marketo as their marketing automation platform, with emphasis on personalization. Using Marketo's real-time personalization across sites enables Rapid7 to personalize a prospect's or buyer's experience, and give them the right information.

Content Marketing and Lead Generation

Most digital marketing is heavily focused on search, both SEO and organic traffic. Rapid7 seeks to provide "rich, really good, valuable content, that make people want to know more about you." To convert web site visitors to prospects, Rapid7 uses a freemium model across a number of solutions, both for trial and free products, so there are different versions of free trials of products that people can download. The freemiums have proven to be a great, natural source of traction that directs people to the Rapid7 web site. (More info on freemiums below.)

For demand programs, Rapid7 uses the content engagement tactics of webinars and white papers. Increased engagement is achieved with Account Based Marketing (see below).

Webcasts: Think in Terms of "Webcast Streams"

How do you avoid webcast fatigue, yet use them effectively?

When asked how Rapid7 avoids webcast fatigue, Allison responds: "We think in terms of webcast streams, because while thought leadership is extremely important, we also see a need in the market, where people just want to understand what you do without having to go through many different channels."

Rapid7 has discovered that a mix of these types of webcasts are very effective:

Live demos, such as 30-minute overviews:

This type of format is very useful if the prospect is not ready to talk to a sales person, and doesn't want to do a lot of the research on their own. The live demo gives the prospect a way to see the product in action (without necessarily going through a sell cycle).

Educational series:

Gives people very specific advice and actual tools they can actually use, rather than just an overview of the market. Levels vary from someone who's just starting out, to experienced CSOs.

Ideally, the webcast speakers are subject matter experts (particularly in-house), with strong backgrounds, deep subject matter knowledge, and industry credibility. Featuring in-house experts has the dual benefit of gaining exposure for your speakers, as well as contributing to your industry's overall community base of knowledge.

Rapid7 has invested in BrightTalk (www.BrightTalk.com) as their webinar platform. Allison claims that BrightTalk enables them to not only give Rapid7 a vehicle to host webinars, but also serves as another channel for Rapid7 to get exposure to potential buyers who may not be familiar with the brand.

Freemiums: Work Great --- But With Caveats

According to Allison, freemiums are very effective because they eliminate all the roadblocks, and give prospects an easy way to sample your product via free tools and trials.

The flip side of the freemium production is the volume of leads who aren't necessarily purchasing the product. This is especially true of markets like the security market, where prospects may be naturally curious, and inclined to make repeat visits to the web site.

To handle the freemium volume, and identify the best leads to hand over to Sales, Rapid uses Infer for lead scoring (now available from Ignite Tech:

https://ignitetech.com/solutions/marketing-and-sales/infer/)

From a scoring standpoint, Rapid7 found that they needed to ignore the "noise" in the system, and not depend on behavioral scoring. For example, a lot of people can click on a lot of web pages, but those actions don't necessarily mean that a lead is ready to convert (they may need more nurturing), or that a lead will ever be ready to convert. Or as Allison advises "we identify who is our ideal buyer, and we focus on the quality of what we send over to Sales."

One other consideration: what is your prospect's likely experience with the freemium? If the prospect's experience with the freemium is bad, someone could say "why would I buy that product?" To guard against that infrequent, but possible, perception, Rapid7 seeks to always improve a prospect's likely freemium experience.

Data Quality - A "Maniacal" Focus

For Rapid7, data hygiene is an extreme priority, particularly due to their extraordinarily high number of leads. In addition to using Infer to score leads (see also BDRs below), Rapid7 uses tools to append certain types of data, such as company and demographic data, to both the contact and account record as they enter into Marketo (their marketing automation tool) and before entry into their CRM system.

It's an ongoing effort --- not "set it and forget it" warns Allison, because buyers and industries change even within a short timespan.

Direct Mail: A (Not-So) Secret Weapon?

According to Allison, direct mail marketing is "making a comeback." Rapid7 employs direct marketing for high-touch campaigns, as well as ABM. In particular, direct mail works for quasi-events, such as promoting lunch-and-learn type of events, or a specific webinar being held just for a single account.

Reporting Tools -- Centralization, and Next Frontier

To provide keep everyone in the loop, Rapid7 uses a centralized reporting and data visualization tool called Domo. Data from Marketo and Rapid7's CRM platform automatically flows in, and Domo enables visualization of different types of data sets, such as:

- How many marketing qualified leads are we generating?

- How are they broken down by different types of categories, different types of campaigns?

- What does the user profile look like?

- Scoring: how do higher lead score impact conversion, opportunity, and deal size? (Hint: higher lead scores generally lead to higher scores across the board.)

- For ABM, there's a separate section of what we look at, ABM can't be measured the same way as inbound marketing (see ABM below).

- For larger accounts: What are we doing to get in front of those accounts?

- How are we driving in new contacts or organizations?

What's next on reporting frontier for Rapid7? According to Allison, it's a better understanding, based on data, on how to better identify the nature of purchasing intent: "One of the things we're also starting to experiment with is the behavioral piece. Who's going to be a more predictable buyer for the sales team? Not only 'this could be a potential buyer,' but also, what are they also doing that's indicating their interests?' Are they ready to be passed off (to Sales), or do we hold back and nurture? We're really trying to get smarter about what we're doing and how we're going to market."

Account Based Marketing (ABM) -- Why Standard Marketing Metrics Won't Work

Rapid7 employs ABM across mid-market enterprise and named accounts. Sales and Marketing work hand-in-hand to grow the business: focus on the larger accounts, get the sales reps into the accounts, help the sales reps to map the accounts, and other activities designed to grow the pipeline and influence the leads in the pipeline. The collaboration between Marketing and Sales results in very specific, high-touch, targeted programs. Goals are reset every quarter, with Marketing aligning very closely with the sales force to ensure successful execution.

What does Allison think is the true key to ABM success? "Really making sure that you have that alignment with your sales team is huge. Along with the tools, and how you're measuring it, that's a big thing... A lot of marketers try to take an ABM approach, but measure it the exact same way they're measuring everything else in marketing. That's really where it can go downhill, because there are some efforts in ABM where you're trying to break in and get awareness of who you are as an organization, but your executive team or your CMO is looking at 'what did that convert to for MQLs or deals or pipeline?' Being able to tell the story, quantify what the goal and the purpose is, and what those results are, is measuring in a completely different way."

Allison also points out that you need to get alignment with Sales, and metrics for success, crystal clear from the beginning. For example: "Are there certain deals where you want to influence that account? A lot of times, if you're doing ABM for large accounts, it's not going to be Marketing that's always going to take that over the finish line. These can be lengthy deal cycles, so really understanding along the journey how do you actually influence that deal? Is it bringing in through your ABM efforts? Is it bringing in new contacts that you've never been in front of before, whether that's through their inbound channel or retargeting or outbound type of marketing programs?"

"Is it really helping with the closing cycle of that deal? Are there certain things you're doing, whether that's in person or higher touch types of programs, that are helping to bring it over the finish line? I think it's understanding when you're setting out your program how you are going to measure at different steps along the way. It all can't be measured the same way."

In other words, you cannot use the standard metrics (conversion from funnel->MQL->lead-> sales qualified lead->opportunity->deal) to develop, execute and measure ABM efforts.

Global Structure -- a Lot of Collaboration

There are US-based marketing programs that perform well in the non-US markets (for Rapid7, the international markets targeted are India and Asia Pacific.) In particular, the inbound freemium channel performs well. Rapid7 localizes the non-US web sites and does a lot of localization to drive people to those sites.

However, despite localization, there is still the need for geographic-specific marketing, and it even extends to ABM efforts. For example, there are certain regions where Rapid7 localizes a lot of the retargeting, and the local marketing team oversees those efforts.

From an overall go-to-market standpoint, the US team will share with the international team what's worked well in the US, and rely on the international team to determine what's going resonate outside the US. More marketing projects tend to be initiated in the US, primarily because the US marketing team is larger. Once a quarter, the US and non-US teams review their joint go-to-market plan, and share what's working in their respective geographies.

BDRs: Uncovering Motivation + A Lens into the Market

In 2012, Rapid7 was a 2-product company, and also offered services. Leads flowed directly to the sales team.

But with a higher volume of leads from freemium and premium content marketing, and a certain amount of "noise" in the system, Marketing ended up throwing a lot of leads at Sales, whereas Sales was focused on closing sales.

Also, with the growing sophistication of their buyer, and an expanded number and type of offerings, Rapid7 needed to stay on top of the different contacts within an organization, and determine how to best interface with them. Allison says "We need to understand exactly what brings prospects to our web site, not just the simplistic view of 'Oh, you downloaded a webcast, what did you think about it?'"

Business Development Representatives (BDRs) were introduced as a bridge between leads produced by Marketing and the Sales team. The BDR team is organized under Sales and is responsible for following up with all inbound leads. Marketing works closely with the BDRs to determine what constitutes a quality lead.

Rapid7 uses the Infer score as a major lever of MQLs. Before a lead is passed to the business development team, each lead is reviewed for:

- Contact Completeness - we use a number of different tools to ensure the quality of the contact info. This type of "lead hygiene" helps create lead quality and predictability.

- Active Interest - We look for people who have taken relevant actions: downloaded a free trial, attended a webcast, hit the "contact us" on a form, downloaded a piece of content.

The Infer score also enables Rapid7 to manage MQL lead production -- different levers are pulled, depending if the marketing team needs to scale back leads, or to let more leads through.

BDRs are extremely effective at getting to the true motivation of prospects. A BDR's follow-up and review is always the final step in determining whether to push a lead to Sales. If it's an opportunity, the BDR passes the lead over to the sales rep. In other words, a human always makes the final determination of a lead is sales-ready.

The BDR program has had the additional benefit of serving as a sales development program. BDRs start with handling inbound calls, progress to outbound calling, and eventually, are promoted into the account executive team. BDRs serve as another outbound contact resource to support account-based marketing (ABM) tactics.

Customer Marketing & Advocacy -- Make it easier for customers to be your advocates

Rapid7 introduced the practice of customer advocacy early on (customer advocacy = enabling and encouraging current customers to write reviews, provide positive references and experience info, and in general, advocate for your organization in social media and other forums.)

Prior to 2016, Rapid7 used an in-house customer advocacy platform, including conducting customer feedback calls, as well as outbound calling to get customers in sync with their U.S. team and their products team. To facilitate Rapid7's "one-to-many" approach, Influitive (advocacy and engagement software) is used to get more customers involved, including customer speaking engagements, customer conferences, and just doing more with customers in general.

Rapid7 also has put significant and growing emphasis into Customer Marketing: how to make customers more successful.

The marketing and sales teams look at everything from how they engage with customers, to helping customers adopt the products they have, encourage purchasing of additional products or services, and last but not least, how to become advocates of Rapid7. All of these aspects comprise the Customer Marketing and Advocacy efforts.

One of Rapid7's greatest successes, according to Allison, is a program called Rapid7Voice. "It's what we call that broader-based customer advocacy program where we're working closely with our customers …on everything from engaging them on how they're using the product to, 'Hey, is anyone interested in participating on a webinar or speaking at a conference?' We've seen huge success there, and I think referrals and customer advocacy is just such a big critical piece of the overall demand and end funnel."

@AlliB1121

Seiya Vogt, Boxed (formerly of Bitly)

Little did we know that when MoC hosted Seiya Vogt, Bitly's former Director of Demand Generation, that the episode would morph into a killer B2B case study. Find out how Bitly manages an insane lead volume with an impressive tech stack of 5 solutions, and a cool strategy that identifies and gets the most out of big money accounts.

Who is Bitly? (And what is their secret sauce?)

Many marketers know Bitly as a link shortener. But by creating links with Bitly's enterprise platform, customers can see how their content is shared across marketing channels, platforms and devices, as well as which content is shared the most.

First, a little background: Bitly is basically a link shortener, especially helpful on Twitter. Bitly's integration partners enable publishing of content across social networks. Bitly can be integrated into other products via an API.

A very cool Bitly feature: You'll see data not only from the links you distribute, but **also when others distribute your links**. (Yes, italics and bold for emphasis. That's the aforementioned secret sauce.)

Most marketers use Bitly to track channel performance. However, performance on an individual basis can also be tracked. In other words, if you send a Bitly link to your list, most typically via an email, each Bitly link is uniquely coded. That means you can tell exactly who uses and/or shares you link.

Links can lead to any landing page, content or promotional. That means that you can see a promotion's performance when it's distributed through your channels, but also when a link is shared outside your list or social media.

For example, let's say that MoC uses a Bitly link to promote this book on Twitter. If anyone in the Twitterverse shares a Bitly link (or if they create their own Bitly link), we'll be able to see how the promotion performs when shared outside of our followers. (Please and thank you for sharing our links.)

The Monster Lead Generator

Bitly uses a link shortener freemium to generate new accounts. The freemium has limited features and is single-user; their enterprise version is multi-user and has a bunch of analytical tools. The freemium is hugely successful, and produces an average of new accounts 4-5K PER DAY, and sometimes as high as 7K.

New freemiums and leads are produced via:

1. Bitly's App (produces a lot of new freemium accounts)

2. Enterprise Version Landing Page: https://bitly.is/2S5bPoI

3. Online Demo Webinar: https://bitly.is/2R6ef5r

4. Organic Search: https://bitly.is/2OxVrPH

SDRs can access data from the source of lead gen to figure out what problems the lead wants to solve. For example, if a lead come in by cell phone, the SDR can explain how Bitly integrates with mobile providers, or point out that Bitly can track marketing efforts across channels.

Bitly uses email as to nurture and inform leads, with a focus on communication with freemium users and newsletters. Email alerts users to new features, apprises leads of Bitly's leadership activities in the analytics space, and of course, converts freemium users to the enterprise platform.

Behold the Bitly Funnel

Bitly has an unusual advantage over other companies, and that's the usage of the Bitly product itself. The Bitly product is so widespread that a key contributor to the funnel is account utilization intelligence. Seiya: "We love when people use the Bitly freemium to create and share links; the more people who the free product, the more data we get." Bitly can also identify who are the best candidates for their enterprise platform version based on freemium usage.

But Bitly didn't always have an ABM strategy. It would take a miracle for Bitly's Sales Development Representative (SDR) outbound team to contact 4-5K new accounts per day, especially without lead scoring or info about the new accounts. Bitly revamped their entire marketing operations to distribute leads more effectively.

New Leads Coding:

Classification: Each lead is assigned a unique lead source based on the call-to-action (CTA) filled out by the lead. Bitly classifies leads based on how the lead enters the funnel.

- Content leads: generated from ebooks, webinars, etc. These leads tend to be top of the funnel; they're high quality, but not ready to talk about the product.

- Product Leads: Leads who have directly expressed interest in the product. They're treated differently than content leads, because they tend to be further down in the funnel, i.e. closer to making a buying decision.

New Lead Hygiene:

RingLead is known for data cleansing and de-duping, so Bitly invested in RingLead to match all new leads against their (at the time) 4+ year-old database.

New Lead Assignment:

Bitly learned that RingLead also has an excellent lead routing system. So at the top of the funnel, immediately after lead de-dupe and cleaning, RingLead is applied.

RingLead routes leads based on named v. non-named account status. Named accounts are Fortune 500 types of organizations; non-named accounts are all other accounts.

Bitly also uses Marketo on top of Salesforce for the distribution of accounts to the sales staff.

Sales Team Management: Named accounts (ABM with a twist)

Named accounts (the Fortune 500 types) are routed directly to a sales rep on the enterprise team, so s/he can immediately contact accounts with the most potential (otherwise, the account goes through an SDR process, which can take days.)

Prior to contact, reps can see info about the individual contact, the overall company, and type of tech the company uses, info which is great for starting relevant conversations.

The Twist: One of the benefits of Bitly's huge market presence is that a lot of their named accounts already have free Bitly accounts. That gives the rep the ability to target relevant messages based on data re: how the account uses Bitly. Also, Bitly already has a map of the content promoted by freemium accounts. Bitly uses their own tool to learn what's being said about the named account, which can be used to initiate a relevant discussion with the account right out of the gate.

Sales Team Management: Non-named accounts

To help use sales resources most efficiently, Bitly scores non-named accounts using Infer. Scoring factors include demographics, past usage of Bitly, similarity to other accounts who use Bitly, and the tech stack used by the account. Bitly also enrich each leads with outside data, to give reps even more info.

Leads earn a score from "A" to "D," with "A" being the highest. Not surprisingly, SDRs generate better results from the "A" leads. If a lead is non-matched, i.e. truly new to the company, not in the CRM system, Bitly's entry touchpoint helps to define what the account is interested in, and therefore, how to assign the account to a SDR on the corporate team.

Bitly's goals include doing more to support ABM and take a more personalized approach at the top of the funnel, such as creating custom pages for named accounts, targeting campaigns toward to specific employees at the company, and developing communication to describe exactly how Bitly can meet the named account's needs.

Marketing Org

Bitly has separate Marketing and Sales departments; Marketing isn't organized under Sales. Marketing partners close with Sales to make sure that the goals and direction are closely aligned. The SDR team, which handles the non-named accounts, works directly with Marketing.

There is a VP of Marketing, a Director of Demand Generation, a Marketing Ops person, and an Email person. There are 2 people on the Content team who work on top-of-the-funnel content, as well as product marketing messaging.

The Stack

To drive a more personalized approach throughout the funnel, Bitly uses these solutions:

Salesforce: Lead Distribution

Marketo: Marketing Automation

Infer: Lead and Account scoring

RingLead: Account De-Duping, Account Routing

ClearBid: Adds data to the back-end

@SeiyaVogt

Justin Mares, FOMO.com, also Kettle & Fire

Traction: How Any Startup Can Achieve Explosive Customer Growth

By Gabriel Weinberg and Justin Mares

https://amzn.to/2PxNV3d

From Justin: "A popular thought at the time that *Traction* was written: all you need for a successful and growing startup is 'build the best product and you'll win.' My co-author, Gabriel Weinberg and I had a lot of issues with that philosophy. We found that there are tons of companies with a great product that solve a certain problem --- but that's just the starting point.

We've grown to believe that startups need be a lot more focused on getting traction as one of the most important things that a business can do."

But...Why You Shouldn't Try to Monetize A Book

According to Justin: "If you look at how much effort it takes to write a book compared to the financial payoff, my co-author and I did a terrible job of ROI. We got tons of advice from people, like 'you guys should do a course. Or you should speaking at conferences or go into consulting.'

But we found that writing a book about startups is truly a passion project (i.e. low $$$). Unless we're going to follow the Tony Robbins monetization route, there's nothing as financially rewarding is just starting a successful business."

(Yes, we realize the irony of including this advice --- in a book. We think it's fair to point out that media companies tend to have a different business model than retail consumer or SaaS companies. As always, evaluate based on your company's distinct economics and opportunities.)

FOMO: Social Proof Technology

Justin shared the story of www.FOMO.com: "My business partner Ryan Culp and I bought Notify (the former name of FOMO), a Shopify application that enables any website to apply the same kind of conversion optimization tools and dynamics that Bookings.com and Hotels.com have on their websites.

If you've ever been on one of those sites and you'll see "alerts", you'll see something like 'Sam just bought this hotel room 40 minutes ago' or '13 people looked at booking this hotel room in the last 2 hours.' This type of social proof drives more conversions by showing the prospect that they're not the only person on this website who's thinking about or acting on a purchase.

Justin also co-owns https://www.KettleAndFire.com with his brother. The site sells bone broth to low-carb and Paleo-type diet followers. Said Justin, "Once I installed FOMO, I saw conversions go up around 30% almost immediately."

"FOMO even applies to content/blog sites; we have a have a couple of bloggers that use it where it plugged into MailChimp. So you could display "Someone from San Francisco, California, just signed up for your newsletter 2 hours ago," or "Someone from Boston, Massachusetts just finished reading this article 40 minutes ago."

After discovering that FOMO increased conversion rates by 30%, Justin Mares was loathe to lose access to the solution when it was time to switch to a new ecommerce platform. He recounts, "We reached out to the developer and said, 'Hey, we're transitioning off of Shopify shortly. Is this solution available on any other platforms? We'd like to keep our conversion gains even after we switch platforms.

The developer said the software wasn't available independent of Shopify. We basically went back and forth, over almost 40 days, and ended up making him an offer. We bought the company from him and rebranded it to Fomo (www.UseFomo.com).

Author's Note: We suggest you take some time to study www.KettleAndFire.com, not just because of the great products, but to see how they use chat technology, pop-ups, etc. Because Justin and his team are actually measuring results, you can have some confidence that these plug-ins are boosting conversion. And be sure to study the home page -- it's almost an entire lesson in SEO by itself.

In the same vein, if you're marketing an SaaS, be sure to checkout www.UseFomo.com to see how they're marketing their solution.

On Content Marketing

"Content marketing is incredibly competitive. And with the way Google works, content marketing is difficult and it takes a relatively long time for your content to get decent rankings on Google. If you're trying to drive traffic in a crowded market -- even if you write the best content out there -- chances are that someone has already written something 80% as good (especially in the marketing tools space.)"

Justin recommends these alternative options to content marketing, especially if you're in a very competitive marketplace:

#1 New Acquisition Channels: Media like FB Live, Periscope, and even YouTube are currently under optimized.

#2 Paid Acquisition --paid advertising opportunities, especially on FB, are better than they've ever been. FB has spent billions of VC dollars and public market capital to acquire almost every individual on the US. For a fraction of revenue you'd make on a customer (for example, just $10), you can reach a specific demographic in a specific area of the country.

"If you have any sort of product that you charge for," explains Justin, "advertising on FB is a

'no-brainer.' Based on what it costs to build incredible pieces of content vs. the small expense of promotion on FB, it's just more difficult for content marketing to make a lot of sense in crowded spaces."

John adds the observation: "You can even discover unexpected correlations that may work. FB will suggest them to you, and you can test them for a tiny fraction of an old-school advertising budget. For example, I did some social media advertising work with Matthew Ebel, a self-published musician, who's done a lot of Piano Rock. We knew Elton

John would be a group to advertise against, but the FB algorithm also suggested Beatles fans; this segment also performed well.

@JayWMares

Social Media, PR and Alternative Media Experts

Jeremy Goldman

Getting to Like: How to Boost Your Personal and Professional Brand to Expand Opportunities, Grow Your Business, and Achieve Financial Success

https://amzn.to/2Ndjthl

In his Marketing Over Coffee interview, Jeremy Goldman generously shared practical advice for using social media to authentically build your personal brand, and avoid the "race to the bottom."

Highlights:

1. Basic business strategy drives your social media choices

This drives the choice of social media channels. For example if you want to drive speaking engagements, you need platforms that will easily support video, i.e. YouTube. If DIY is in your target mix, Pinterest needs to be part of your strategy. Your social media focus will also drive your optimal visuals and type of content --- for example, long form v. short form writing, video or live form video, etc.

2. Building your Personal Brand

Most senior execs concentrate on Twitter and Linkedin. It's not unusual for senior execs to lag in taking full advantage of social media, because they depend on their resume to do the heavy lifting.

- Use Twitter and LinkedIn to the Max: When focusing on LinkedIn and Twitter, keep up-to-date with any new capabilities – for example, when LinkedIn allowed high resolution photos, people still left up their old low res photos, which look odd.

- Highlight Accomplishments in Your Profile: Don't hide your key achievements in your resume; feature them in your LinkedIn profile.

- If you're on Twitter, tweet consistently: Twitter management is an important way to bolster your persona, either because you may be on the market, or you may want to become more valuable to your company. A paucity of tweets is not the way to go.

- Junior People: Start building your brand right away: Look for opportunities to perform side projects that relate to what you want to get known for. For example, you can design a Tumblr to show off great design skills. By focusing your professional social media on where you want to go, you'll ultimately gain you more control.

3. Tools: Manage "Flitter"

All those social media platforms are so tempting. Try to specialize in just a few platforms in the beginning. It's better to become a master of some platforms than to dabble in all platforms.

4. Content: The Great Differentiator

Content matters. You want to break through the clutter, and you want to do it authentically. Don't look for shortcuts --- there are lots of other smart people on the internet, and they have already found and leveraged the content creation shortcuts you think you've discovered. Put out something great instead of consistently putting out so-so stuff.

5. Competition: When everybody zigs, you should zag

It's OK to pay attention to your competition and take note of what they do, but don't become a weakened, watered-down version of competitors. It's possible to become a decent lookalike by doing what your competition does, and doing it 1% better. But the better strategy is to figure out what is missing.

@jeremarketer

Tim Street

Authentic/Showable Media

John likes to check in with Tim Street periodically to get Tim's take on all things podcasting and VR. Tim has been in the entertainment and advertising industries, keeping tabs on the rise of new media, so his insights always merit attention.

Podcasting is on the Rise

The IAB is taking podcasting seriously:

https://adexchanger.com/digital-audio-radio/podcasting-inches-toward-better-measurement-new-iab-guidelines/

Measuring Podcasting

Overall, the community supports a standard methodology to provide accurate download statistics, so that the advertising community can get reliable statistics. Podtrac is becoming the industry standard for podcast measurement, similar to how Nielsen or ComScore provide viewership data. Podtrac gets permission to release podcast listener stats from the podcaster, and that's how they put together the list of top podcasts.

Freebie Alert: You can use the Podtrac measurement system for your own podcast free by asking your own hosting company (like Libsyn or Blubrry) to activate the PODTRAC measurement system. You'll get podcast stats for subsequent episodes.

The Reality of Virtual Reality

It's still not easy to produce VR. It's like the early days of podcasting and web video, when you had to do everything yourself because tools are under development.

And there still isn't a big audience for VR, except for video games. It's the old adage: whenever there's a technological advance in entertainment, spectacle comes first, then story. VR excels at spectacle. There are some great stories being told in the top video games, but video games are mostly spectacle. X-rated technology also has a following, so VR will be popular there as well.

Tim advises "I always tell people that any technology isn't a real form of entertainment until Apple's involved. As of now, Apple doesn't have a VR marketplace; industry reports that one may be up and running in 2020. When you go to the iTunes store or the app store, they're not pushing big VR experiences yet. There are VR apps for the iPhone and you can watch those on Google Cardboard or you could get the View-Master VR starter pack:" https://www.amazon.com/View-Master-Virtual-Reality-Starter-Pack/dp/B011EG5HJ2

Tim's impressions of VR: "At SXSW, I had a bad experience with a car company's driving simulator, which was a vomit-mobile. But after I tried some other VR experiences, I was super impressed. A lot of the VR experiences are still experimental and not the highest level of quality. If you look back to the early days of TV or VHS, everyone loved the new access to content, but the viewing quality wasn't optimal.
Currently, you'd never want to shoot a feature film on VHS, because the gap between VR and what consumers are used to

at the movies is so great that VR feels like an inferior experience. But recent VR live action experiences are on VHS-type quality level."

"Part of the reason VR isn't ready for mass adoption yet; the technology isn't sufficiently powerful. New cameras are being developed to support VR, with major players like Nokia getting into the space. A lot of folks use GoPros, and chain them together to create VR experiences. But it's still hard to shoot footage that's high quality, and then edit that footage into an end result that can be consumed easily. To shoot at the optimal rate, 8k at 120 frames a second, still requires spending thousands on cameras and gear. My suggestion to aspiring VR creators: experiment, but don't create your masterpiece in VR yet. (Unless you're developing a video game. That's a whole different scenario.)"

"Another reason for lack of mass adoption is that the general public is just starting to get their head around VR. All the VR insiders know where to get good VR footage and experiences. But most people aren't aware of any venues where they can go to have VR experiences."

"There're some people who are true pioneers in the VR space, and have contributed mightily to its progress. But if you wait a couple of years, there's going to be a new tool set that's so much easier and less expensive. I'm thankful that there are talented people that are willing to do the work and bring their visions to life in VR."

"In terms of content for any of these mediums, I like content that draws you into a story. We've seen video bloggers take off and do a great job at building audiences.

There's one case where someone on Vimeo created a web series about a marijuana delivery service that's now on HBO.

(Here's a link to "High Maintenance": https://www.hbo.com/high-maintenance)"

"But I'm more excited about podcasting than video. YouTube is in the fledgling stages of developing series, but we don't have a Sopranos of YouTube yet."

Editor's note: YouTube has come a long way since John's discussion with Tim.

Check out these articles YouTube series worth watching, and upcoming series with major star power:

Top 10 Family-Friendly YouTube Series

https://www.deseretnews.com/article/865692686/10-family-friendly-YouTube-series-that-are-just-as-good-as-real-TV-shows.html

Top 10 Black YouTube Series

https://blavity.com/10-black-youtube-series-that-you-should-binge-watch-this-weekend

Robert Downey Jr. to host a YouTube Show on AI:

https://mashable.com/2018/05/15/robert-downey-jr-youtube-series/#uZk0jMsh.PqC

@1TimStreet

Tom Webster

Edison Research

Podcasting Insights

Tom Webster is the Publisher of **The Infinite Dial** report by from Edison Research: http://www.edisonresearch.com/infinite-dial-2018/

This annual report examines how & why humans use technology, based on telephone surveys, including reaching people by mobile phone.

Podcasting Goes Exponential

While podcasting has grown steadily over the past decade, it caught fire with "Serial" https://serialpodcast.org/ (John describes "Serial" as the first podcasting 'water cooler moment'.)

When the "Serial" series ended, people looked for other podcasts to follow, so there was a multiplier effect to podcast listenership.

Podcast Discovery

Right now, there isn't a good podcast directory. There's iTunes, but podcast discovery tends to be content-driven, i.e. listeners discover podcasts within content they're reading. Most listeners click and immediately listen to a show.

That's one of the reasons that social media is vital to podcast discovery and listenership. People who are niche celebrities with a substantial social media following, e.g. Adam Carolla from PodCastOne https://www.podcastone.com/Adam-Carolla-Show can simply post or tweet a link to their most recent show to get people to tune in.

Selling Podcasting to Advertisers

Podcasting has not yet hit the audience threshold needed before the space can support the type of 3rd party audience measurements used for television, radio and digital. To support brand advertising, advertisers need to know who's listening to podcasts, and to see evidence podcasting's effectiveness in advertising large brands.

To date, podcast advertising has been primarily direct response advertising, or is advertising that underwrites public media podcasts. Insistence upon performance-based measurement, such as conversions or sales, has limited the medium's growth. Even the name, podcasting, is out-of-date because hardly anyone uses iPods anymore. (John loves the phrase Tom coined: "audio on demand".) Podcasting needs to go after the $15+ billion audio (mostly radio) advertising market.

Many podcasting professionals believe podcast advertising should command a premium, because of the trust that people place in the hosts. When a host reads an advertising spot, and conveys their conviction for the product, it's far better than anonymous advertising in most other media. As an industry, podcasting needs to be able to quantitatively justify the premium for the intimacy and indirect endorsement effect of podcast advertising.

While there may be a cap on the time available for podcasting overall (and hence, a limit to podcasting advertising space), there is no cap on an individual's desire to consume content that they want, where and when they want to consume it.

Show First

Tom explains: "There was a time when advertising or promoting your show as a podcast made a lot of sense, but it's gotta be show first. You build the show first and then people will figure out ways to consume it."

Two Big Examples (Revenue and Audience)

NPR started with content that most people know (e.g. Fresh Air), and made it available on demand. They also have the ability to cross promote new podcasts, as cross promotion is one of the most effective vehicles for enabling new podcasts to gain traction.

PodCastOne launched with celebrities with built-in audiences, even celebrities that aren't known predominantly online. For example, it's easy to justify building a custom studio for laying down some podcast tracks with Shaquille O'Neal, because of his huge name recognition and social following.

Corporate and Business Podcasts

Tom on business podcasts: "There's always going to be companies wanting to build relationships with like-minded people, or prospects interested buying or their product or service. But product-centered content is NOT the way to do it. The idea is to provide entertainment that's brought to you by the company sponsor. In some cases, there may even be product placement. That's an incredibly powerful way for a brand to advertise."

@webby2001

Customer Perception Virtuosos

Jay Baer
Hug Your Haters

https://amzn.to/2yBl6wY

Youtility: Why Smart Marketing is About Help, Not Hype

https://amzn.to/2SpYKXi

If you think that customer service is primarily a cost-center, pay close attention to Jay's hard-core research into customer service. The metrics don't lie. And with the proliferation of online reviews and social media, Customer Service has been disrupted, the same way that Marketing has been disrupted.

Is "Speed" the Killer App?

Well, sure. Businesses that respond more quickly to customers, in any media, have an inherent advantage.

But is the speed of reply the most important factor in customer satisfaction?

Jay collaborated with Tom Webster of Edison Research to perform a study on the science of complaint. They surveyed of thousands of customers, and found that while speed is an important factor, it's not *the* most important factor.

#1 Factor: SHOW UP

Jay and Tom discovered that as many as ⅓ of complaints are never addressed. Almost all unanswered complaints appear in online, public-facing media: social media, review sites, discussions boards and forums. The real differentiator in perceived customer service value is to answer every complaint, in every media, and every time.

The study also revealed that that answering just one customer complaint can increase a customer's loyalty by 25%. The reverse is also true; when you don't answer customer complaints, it always decreases customer loyalty and advocacy.

Jay reports, "Being able to solve a problem in one contact is a big priority for most customers (so they don't waste time.) But from a customer loyalty and advocacy perspective, you get 75-80% of the credit just for responding to their complaint. Resolving the problem produces another 15-20% of credit.

Or as Jay says: "Haters are not your problem. Ignoring them is."

All the Channels, All the Time

You may have already noticed that customer want to interact in the channels that they prefer, instead of the channels that the business prefers. Traditional customer service channels, such as phone and email, have been augmented by Facebook and Twitter. Channel proliferation has extended to FB Messenger, WhatsApp, WeChat, and specialized customer service-based apps. Now businesses need to be responsive in 10-12 forms of media for optimal results.

Sanity Tip: Yes, you can make the decision to limit your company's number of social media channels. But if you do, you'll need to let customers know that you're not going to respond via a specific media. If you're going to open up yourself to comments and ridicule, which is ever-present in social media, you have to commit the resources to field that commentary.

"Welcome to Lake Woebegone, Where ... All the Children are Above Average"

Garrison Keillor probably wasn't thinking of customer service when he coined this witticism, but there's a discrepancy between how businesses and customers perceive customer service quality. Forrester found that 80% of businesses say that they deliver superior customer service. However, the customers of those same businesses say that only 8% deliver superior customer service. Of course, it's often the execs in charge of customer service who measure and judge their own performance. No one has ever gone into a meeting and said "we don't have excellent customer service."

Also, Jay saw discrepancies in customer perception creep into marketing. For example, a business might present the message that "we're the 'neighborhood bar and grill,'" but that's not necessarily the perception of their customers.

On-Stage vs. Off-State Haters

"On-Stage Haters" are younger, more tech savvy, and more active on social media. They complain in public: on social media, on consumer review sites like Yelp and TripAdvisor, and on vertical sites like Angie's List. In B2B, they complain on sites G2 Crowd, SpiceWorks, TrustRadius, and other industry discussion boards and forums.

Off-Stage Haters are a little older, a little less tech savvy, and a little less social media friendly. They complain "in private" using legacy channels, such as phone and email. About 90% of the time, they expect and want an answer. But the advocacy effect achieved by the business responsiveness is minor, because the complainer expects a response.

How to Make Complaints on Social Media Work for You

Business tends to think of Twitter as the customer service part of social media; many companies have specific customer service Twitter handles, such as @CompanyCustomerCare or @CompanyHelp

But research reveals that only 17% of complaints are lodged through Twitter. The vast majority of complaints --- approximately 71% -- of complaints are lodged on Facebook. That's primarily because Facebook is so much larger than Twitter. The complainers are not necessarily expecting a reply from the business on Facebook; usually, they're seeking group sympathy. But if a business does answer complaints on Facebook, Twitter, TripAdvisor or Yelp, the business achieves a huge advocacy advantage, because the complainers are surprised that their complaints have been found and acknowledged by the company.

Key lesson: You should acknowledge a complaint, empathetically, in social media, so that both the customer and onlookers can see that you've responded quickly and appropriately. But it is best to resolve a specific problem with the customer offline, via phone or email.

Also, follow Jay Baer's Rule: "Reply Only Twice." Never reply more than twice to any one person in any single conversation online. Following that rule limits the number of times you'll "take a hit" from the complainer, so you'll save time.

The New Call Center

At the time of Jay's research, about ⅔ of complaints took place off-stage. However, off-stage complaining is rapidly shifting to on-stage, because it's so much easier to complain via social media and apps than to take the time to write an email or to call. Companies need to reconsider the term "call center," and reconfigure their expectations and resources.

For example, WhatsApp is not well-known in the US, but it has over a billion users internationally. It seems to have transcended the "line" between public and private contact, replacing email and even the phone with real-time access.

In New Delhi, India, the traffic police have a dedicated WhatsApp number. In India, 71% of the population uses social media for customer service, so it's a natural progression for citizens to reach out to the police online. Jay: "Users of WhatsApp are encouraged to send audiovisual complaints of traffic violations, unauthorized parking, faulty traffic signals and other traffic-related issues. Someone even reported a crime by sending a video of it to police via WhatsApp."

An inspector and about 25 police officers monitor the WhatsApp helpline 24/7, handling about 12,000 contacts per month. Of those contacts, about 9% were actionable complaints."

"Listening Software" to the Rescue -- With Caveats

"Listening" is the process of an organized and real-time search for anytime your company is mentioned online. Listening capabilities need to address more than just the obvious mentioned on Facebook and Twitter. You need to find the mentions of your business in places where customers don't think you're going to reply.

Listening software can help, but be aware that solutions differ based on complexity, geography, and other factors. Ideally, you'll use software that operates horizontally within the support department. Often, companies experience a gap between "on-stage" and "off-stage" complaints: one software platform will power off-stage complaint resolution (email and phone), and a different software package will handle social media complaints -- and the two solutions don't talk to each other. Often, customers will call, be dissatisfied with the response and then tweet. The person who answers the tweet doesn't know that the customer previously called, as there's no consistency of data, or historical record of contact. That gap can create a lot of service missteps. Larger companies are using software packages that enable seamless movement between channels, because that's how customers behave.

At the entry level, solutions such as Hootsuite are useful. At the top end, the big players have solutions from the big CRM players such as Oracle, and Salesforce. There are also customized solutions from vendors such as HP, Clarabridge, Aspect Software and Conversocial. Customer Service tech is "going crazy" similar to how MarTech experienced explosive growth previously.

Yes, Virginia, Customer Service IS a Revenue Center

KLM Royal Dutch Airline is one of Jay's customer service favorites. They employ 150+ full-time people answering over 50-60,000+ customer questions and complaints per week, in 14 languages, 24/7. While performing customer service, including sending customers links, etc., they sold over $25MM of airline tickets in 2015.

KLM has a unique customer service culture: the "un" copy and paste culture. They empower their team to work "off script" and give the team permission to take advantage of opportunities to improve customer service, and even more broadly, the customer experience.

For example, like all airlines, people leave stuff on planes. Initially, KLM used this lost item procedure:

1. Flight cleaning crew finds a left behind item (like headphones, book, etc.)

2. The crew writes the flight # and the seat where the item's been found on a sticky note.

3. The crew tweets about the physical item and puts it on a desk.

4. If someone calls or tweets about the lost item, the customer is given a link to an online claim form requiring detailed ID info.

5. Airline personnel locates lost item from the desk, and returns the item.

This return process took days, was a hassle, and most people didn't get their stuff back.

A KLM team member, without asking permission or a broad-based corporate imperative, went to all the team members in Amsterdam --- instituted a new process: "If you find something, text me." The team member walked around the airport with an iPad. Many times, because Amsterdam is a hub, people were waiting for the next flight. The team member would look up the manifest, get the lost item, and return the item to the customer at the gate of their next flight, even before the customer realized that the item had been lost!

@JayBaer

Kate Edwards

Author of **Hello: And Every Little Thing That Matters**

https://amzn.to/2qe25Mr

Kate Edwards is the Principal of Kate Edwards Consulting LLC (http://www.kateedwardsconsulting.com/about-1/), and a 30-year veteran of the hospitality business, creating service and training programs for customer-focused businesses. She also works as an executive coach to help entrepreneurs, chefs, and managers develop their ideas, accomplish their goals, and realize their full potential.

One of things we noticed from Kate's interview is how thoroughly the idea of customer experience permeates all of her perspective and advice. As Kate observes: "I've noticed through my career is that service isn't just pouring water and pulling out a chair. It's the entire guest experience... the full, tactile experience that they're having... how does it feel to sit in the chair, how does it feel to walk in the door?"

Cleanliness = Service

If you have responsibility for conducting or evaluating customer feedback surveys, recognize that customers might misinterpret random impressions of your company as service. For example, when it comes to facilities (hotels, restaurants, other physically-based businesses), customers expect the premises to be absolutely spotless. Customers will notice dust in the air vents, on the upper leaves of plants, and even the cleanliness of a parking garage. All these seemingly small items demonstrate attention to detail. All of these impressions can and will be incorporated into your service rating.

Service-Oriented people - Are They Born or Made?

According to Kate, it's both -- a job candidate needs to be inwardly motivated toward helping people. But service skills are trainable, like a muscle, and can be improved over time.

Service Education is a Social Act

It's much harder to learn customer service on an individual basis. It's much easier to learn it in a team setting. Team training, and any sort of team meetings before an event or at the beginning of the day, give people a chance to "warm-up" and try things out with people they know. Examples range from presenting the today's special deals to sharing innovations in the company. Because presenting and sharing is such a big part of service, warming up with the team makes it easier to perform with strangers that will be encountered during the work day.

How to Create A Culture of Service

First off, you must make the culture "come to life," every day. The company owners and managers need to lead the way and "walk the walk," so that the team and the customers can see the culture in action.

Kate is a firm believer in creating, and as importantly, living by a mission statement. Support your mission statement with a set of Core Values you can reference in your daily communications, updates, any employee newsletters, etc. Core values can even be displayed online (here's a link to a page on Zappos dedicated to company culture and Core Values: https://www.zappos.com/core-values)

The Killer Interview Question

"Tell me a story."

Of course, not every customer service applicant has a story in their hip pocket. Interview questions that can help an applicant tell a story:

"Tell me about the time you stood up for a colleague."

"Tell me a time about the time you solved a problem."

"How did you innovate something on your last job?"

Kate has found that if a service job candidate can engage her by building a story, it's likely that they'll be able to engage a stranger in a sales encounter, over the phone or in person. Keeping someone's attention is a pretty good precursor to being good at service.

Look for "Energy Out"

Service requires a lot of energy, because the candidate has to continuously think about and reach out to people. If the candidate doesn't have high energy and intensity, service is really going to drag them down. Enthusiasm for people and a positive "vibe" also counts.

"Service as Marketing": Applies to Any Customer-Facing Business

All businesses, even pure internet businesses, are customer-facing businesses. Service boils down to the opportunity to touch a prospect or a customer. Even on the internet, you have an opportunity to draw people in, keep them on your site, which is an extension of your service. Whether it's online or in-person, service is marketing, because people remember and share positive experiences.

Building a Customer Service Map

The Customer Service Map is not a metaphor for set of service procedures.

You need to literally go through a relatively tedious, detail-oriented mapping process.

Moreover, you need to map not just the physical process, but also the emotional outcomes.

For example, what are all the steps a customer takes as they enter your facility -- not just the physical steps, but also, what does the customer experience and feel every steps of the way? What does your company want to be the experience to be? How will the customer's impression will be activated by the guest experience?

Document all of the physical and experiential details in your customer map, and then make adjustments to achieve the customer impressions and actions that you want.

Technology Does Take the Place of Talking to Customers

There's some cool technology that enables quick and efficient ratings of service. An example includes restaurant "Happy or Not" kiosks that are placed on a table after a meal, or at a restaurant's cashier. The kiosk displays 4 smiley faces, so the customer can easily pick a smiley face rating of 1-4.

While the technology is cool, and probably gets a 90%+ utilization rate, it is an oversimplified system. The ratings don't really tell you what worked, and what didn't work for the customer. You need to "get in there" and talk to your customers to find out what's really going on.

@ServiceDefined

Daniel Lemin

Manipurated: How Business Owners Can Fight Fraudulent Online Ratings and Reviews

https://amzn.to/2Cepq9C

That this is one of the few podcasts that where MoC didn't discuss all the topics we could have. John's personal copy of Manipurated is 100% marked up in red ink. The book is full of useful info on how to deal with your online reputation: rating-and-review sites, aggressive sales reps and pitches to advertise on those sites, reputation management companies, negative reviews, and advertising on Yelp. Also a ton of listings: rating and review tracking services.

If you, as a consumer, depend on Yelp for restaurant and other ratings, or if you use Amazon reviews as a stand-in for Consumer Reports, this book will make you much better at spotting fake and "paid for" reviews.

If you're a brick and mortar business, before you invite any Yelp Elite Squaders to check out your business, be sure to read this article from MarketingLand:

https://marketingland.com/businesses-need-know-yelp-elite-program-202793

The Review Sandwich: How Customers Really See Online Reviews

The most common question is "I got this really bad review, what do I do?"

Daniel's response: "No need to panic. The good news is that people look at reviews holistically. They don't single out the bad review. If all reviews are good, it's suspicious. Consumers would rather see a "review sandwich.""

According to *Manipurated*, this is the structure of a "Perfect Review Sandwich":

Great Review

Great Review

Amazing Review

OK Review

Bad Review

OK Review

Great Review

It's natural to be sensitive to your first negative review -- but it's suspicious to consumers if you have NO bad reviews! Every business has a bad review. If there are a couple of bad reviews sprinkled into mostly good and great reviews, it adds credibility to your reviews overall.

It's how you handle a bad review that matters

1. Make it a Habit: First off, look at reviews regularly, just as if you'd be reviewing your inventory. Once a month, or even once a week, is too infrequent. Your customers submit reviews 24/7, so you'd better keep up with them. (If you can't do it yourself,

Manipurated provides a comprehensive listing of tracking services, and surveillance specialists.)

2. Respect the reviews: There's a tendency to trivialize the review platforms, but recognize that the reviews are written by actual customers.

3. De-Personalize bad reviews: Don't take reviews personally. That's hard to do, particularly for a small business. If you get a bad review, here's a mantra you should recite and follow:

    a. Stop, Drop & Roll (It's the same mantra you should use in case of a fire)

    b. Stop - yourself from a knee-jerk reaction.

    c. Drop - the attitude. Don't take it personally.

    d. Roll - with the punches. Bad reviews happen.

4. Acknowledge the Reviewer's feelings: Many people just want confirmation that their complaint has been noticed. Respond by acknowledging the reviewer's concern, using as neutral language as possible. (Useful phrases: "not as expected" or "disappointed")

Caveat: If a negative reviewer goes overboard by exaggerating the circumstances, or using dramatic or provoking language, do not respond in kind with overly defensive or descriptive language. Most people will recognize an overly negative review; let the questionable judgment of the reviewer be the focus by giving a short, non-emotional reply.

What About Fake Reviews?

Fake reviews, positive and negative, are pervasive. When Yelp went public, they cited that they screen out 25% of reviews as fraudulent or fake (it appears they have algorithms to identify non-legit reviews.) Amazon sued about 1,200 people who were writing fake reviews for hire. A MIT researcher has identified 20% of reviews on Yelp as fake. Anonymous reviewers is the core problem.

Is legal action possible?

From **Manipurated**: "Some business owners have used the courts to force the rating-and-review sites to address inaccurate or fake content. Many lawsuits involved attempts to force a site to unmask a reviewer's identity. Thus far, the courts have generally ruled in favor of consumers rather than businesses on the grounds of not limiting free speech."

However, there's been some productive legal action. An individual was found guilty and sentenced to 15 years in prison for extortion: threatening to post fraudulent comments and creating negative reviews online if the victim did not pay him a certain sum of money. In other words, a one-star reviewer on Yelp. Here's the story:

https://www.justice.gov/usao-ndtx/pr/search-engine-optimizer-sentenced-more-three-years-federal-prison-extorting-money-local

@DanielLemin

Bonus Chapter - AI Goofs

Why AI Won't Steal Your Job This Week

"Good morning. Welcome to Martini Over Coffee."

A tough way to start the morning.

Despite the amazing things that AI can do, John does not fear our impending robotic overlords: "I've realized that AI still needs to be taught like a human. Since most American companies can't do anything for more than 3-4 years, AI is going to have a hard time getting beyond the intelligence of a 4-year-old kid that gets dropped off and forgotten."

Here's our proof that AI is not ready for world domination: our "best of" AI transcription goofs. (When artificial intelligence tried to translate MoC podcasts into usable English. And failed.)

This is Marketing Over Coffee...

The MoC podcast has a pre-recorded intro, which means the AI will always get it right. Right?

Wrong. Correct intro:

John: "Good morning and Welcome to Marketing over Coffee. I'm John Wall"

Chris: "and I'm Christopher Penn."

The AI:

"Welcome to Marketing over Coffee. I'm John Wall Oven."

"I'm John Long Time Christopher."

"Welcome to Mark Me Over Coffee."

"Macy's Marketing over Coffee with Christopher Penn. And John."

"This is Marketing over Coffee with Christopher Penn and John was the morning walk into Marketing over Coffee."

"I'm John Wall by Christopher Penn."

Chris's Name = AI's Delight

The AI got John's name wrong. A lot.

But not nearly as wrong as frequently or as creatively as Chris' name:

"Christopher Penn logs at Christopher ESPN dot com"

"I'm Christopher About."

"Marketing over Coffee with Christopher Pyne.

"I'm Christopher Tippett."

(We have no idea how the AI came up with this one.)

"I'm Gretchen Rubin"

(Scout's honor, we're not making this up.)

Chris's Stripper Names

We thank the AI for these revelations:

"I'm Krista Preven."

"I'm Christine Romans."

"I'm Chrysalis, a developer that had to become a marketing guy."

Sex and AI

Leave it to AI to find innuendo and smut:

"You know, it's funny. I'm a stack and flow with my sister."

[s/b "Stack and Flow with Sean Zinsmeister"]

"It was mostly me to learning how to make a girl calls in PHP"

[s/b "make cURL calls"]

Now with More Idioms!

AI is not expert in figures of speech

"If you can't spot the soccer at the poker table, it's you."

[s/b "If you can't spot the sucker at the poker table, it's you."]

"What else are these infants talking about?"

[s/b "what else are these influencers talking about"]

"Why would you buy some kind of adnate newspaper?

Now With More Proper Names!

It's not fair to mock AI's transcription of proper names.

Or is it?

"Those are reported on in play, Belle."

[s/b Playbill]

"I'm the founder of accurate."

[s/b founder of AccuRev]

"David Mamet Scott"

[s/b David Meerman Scott]

Now With More Proper Names Attempts!

Sometimes the AI tried to create proper names. And failed.

"The Cereal Effect"

[s/b The Serial Effect]

"I expected the rumor Phil tell-all."

[s/b "the rumor-filled tell-all"]

"Some pieces require more technical experience than Ben."

[s/b "more technical experience than your average marketer."]

We're not sure how the AI translated "average marketer" into Ben.

Sorry, Ben.

Now with More Sage Advice!

Taking MoC wisdom to the next level:

"Do not wish to a nickel."

[s/b "Do not waste a nickel."]

"That's one of the furious left where humans provide value"

[s/b "That's one of few areas left where humans will provide value"]

"You can get a good deal if you start with a ruble sharing service first."

[s/b "You can get a good deal if you start with a room sharing service first."]

Now with More Nature!

"Helps you bundle them into groups of forest."

[s/b "Helps you bundle them so far as"]

"I didn't do a full bird when I'd heard he passed."

[s/b "I didn't do a full burn when I'd heard he had passed."]

"These test cases are proof of concepts of predictive sales and marketing within fur."

[s/b "with Infer" Infer was a MoC sponsor, purchased by ESW Capital]

Now With More Events!

The AI had fun inventing event names

(IBM, take note. 13/10 would attend event with revised name.)

"We have Hubbs Spots Inbound"

[s/b "HubSpot's Inbound"]

"IBM World of Watsup"

[s/b "IBM World of Watson"]

Now With More Show Notes!

MoC Podcast Show Notes were fair game for the AI:

"There's a link in the Schoenaerts."

[s/b There's a link in the Show Notes]

"There's a link in the showmance."

[s/b There's a link in the Show Notes]

Contrary to rumors, Chris and John's relationship is platonic and collegial.

Now with More Seth Godin!

Maybe the AI got nervous in Seth's presence?

"Well, the NBA is doing better than ever, we've won 14 sessions."

[s/b "Well, the altMBA is doing better than ever, we've run 14 sessions."]

"...that explain the relationship between Don Corleone and the undertaker bonus Sarah..."

[s/b "the undertaker Bonasera"]

"The Marketing seminar, Casa 10th as much"

[s/b "The Marketing Seminar costs a 10th as much]

"A term that's been kicked around is D massive vacation."

[s/b "demassification"]

Now with More Body Parts!

Looks like the AI is down with Jeffrey Dahmer:

"You still need a human foot."

[s/b "need a human for it."]

"Google created, had three eyes"

[s/b "Google created 3 AIs "]

"There's less need to do money laundering when you can hide your income from the ears."

[s/b "from the IRS"]

Now with More Monk, Jay, and Christopher Pyne!

Our standard MoC ending:

You've been listening to Marketing Over Coffee. Christopher Penn blogs at ChristopherSPenn.com. Read more from John J. Wall at JW5150.com. The Marketing over Coffee theme song is called Mellow G by Fonkmasters, and you can find it on Music Alley at Mevio, or follow the link in our Show Notes.

We'll leave you with the AI's most mangled interpretation of the podcast close:

"You've been listening to Monk getting Coffee. Christopher Pyne blogs. Christopher Pyne, don't come more for Jay. Don't comb. The marketing recovery theme song is called Mellow Monsters and you can find it need to Kylie for photos. Them think you know share notes."

Made in the USA
San Bernardino, CA
22 April 2019